Par

As she strolled through the aisles picking up items of food – feeling them, quickly tasting a grape – her eyes were drawn to his through a gap between the pasta and the cereal. Dark, sensitive eyes that held a hint of mischief. For what seemed like an eternity, he stood there holding her gaze. Then he turned and walked away; leaving her shaken and slightly breathless.

She hesitated for a second, her concentration momentarily broken. "Now, what was it I wanted?" she said aloud. Then she remembered – fruit for the kids' packed lunches for the coming week. She picked up a bag of apples; contemplated a bunch of bananas. But fruit was the last thing on her mind.

All she could see were those eyes...

Food for Love

Grace and Sonia Bailey

Photographs by
Gloria Nicol

ARP
Angela Royal Publishing

Food for Love

Get ready!

When you are getting ready to create single-handed the perfect romantic feast for your date, remember that it can be a lot of fun to cook your romantic meal together – preparing the ingredients, sharing the tasks, tasting. You can shower or bathe while the meal cooks – you could bathe together if you feel so inclined! Prepare yourselves with as much care as you have lavished on your meal, then share a glass of wine before you finally enjoy your culinary creation.

7 steps to the Perfect Evening

Step 1 Select the partner of your choice and pin them down to a firm dinner date. Pick a time when you won't be interrupted by distracting phone calls or unwelcome visitors so you can give your guest your undivided attention.

Step 2 Prepare yourself well in advance of your guest's arrival. Take time over your appearance and choose your outfit with care. Ideally, you should wear clothes you feel comfortable in but at the same time look like you've made an effort, when dressing for your date. A long soak in a hot tub sprinkled with aromatic oils can help to dispel any last minute nerves, leaving you feeling relaxed and ready to enjoy yourself.

Step 3 Mingle soft, mellow lighting with discreet background music and a table laid for two, to create an atmosphere of warm intimacy.

Step 4 Blend a light starter, a succulent main course and a tantalising dessert to produce the perfect lovers' banquet. For your convenience, a selection of set menus has been put together in this book, featuring meals that are easy to make and absolutely delicious!

Step 5 Nibble on a selection of tasty titbits as a prelude to the main meal when your guest arrives. A light buffet of tempting finger food will whet your appetites for the delights to come!

Step 6 While away some time in relaxed conversation over pre-dinner drinks. 'Nirvana', a wickedly tangy cocktail made with tequila, grenadine and lemon juice, will warm the heart and tease the palate.

Step 7 Devour, at your leisure, an exquisite dinner served in the perfect setting.

Round off the meal with fresh ground coffee, your favourite liqueur and... the rest is up to you!

Enjoy!!!

Remember...

♥ that... vegetables and salads can be peeled and cut to be steamed and dressed nearer the time. Store them in plastic freezer bags in the refrigerator.

♥ that... vegetables should be steamed until cooked but firm to avoid loss of valuable nutrients and to allow them to retain good colour and texture. Always use a sharp knife to cut vegetables.

♥ to... prepare the food in good time and always check that foods which take a long time to cook, are well on the way before your guest arrives.

♥ to... use a timer so that you can leave the food to cook unattended. A ruined dinner could spoil your evening!

♥ to... select and iron your tablecloths and napkins. Set the table beforehand not forgetting table lighting, (ie candles, kerosene lamp) flowers and napkin holders.

♥ to... choose and prepare serving bowls, plates, glasses and cutlery. If using hot-plates, ensure that they are plugged in and switched on. Monitor the heat levels so as not to overcook the food in case your guest is late.

♥ to... wash-up as you go along – a romantic evening with dirty dishes and pans scattered around is definitely not appealing!

♥ to... set up the coffee and cups and warm the plates.

♥ to... offer your guest a drink and appetiser on arrival to 'break the ice'.

Then... have a *Wonderful Evening!*

Wines

Selecting wines to serve with the meal is almost as important as the food selection. Below is a guide for you to follow, but also remember to consider the taste of the foods to be served.

Starters	Dry or Medium White
Soups	Dry White or Red, Sherry, Madeira
Fish	Medium White or Light Red
Red Meat/Game	Full-bodied Red
White Meat	Full-bodied Red or White
Cheeseboard	Red or Port
Dessert	Sweet White
	Mineral Water

Culture Check!

Your guest could be...

♥ **Hindu**
   eats no beef
   is mostly vegetarian
   rarely eats fish
   drinks no alcohol
   fasts at certain periods in time

♥ **Sikh**
   eats no beef
   meat must be killed in a humane way
   drinks no alcohol

♥ **Rastafarian**
   eats no animal products but drinks milk
   only eats 'Ital' food, no added salt
   drinks no coffee or alcohol

♥ **Jewish**
   eats only 'kosher' meat
   only eats fish with scales and fins

♥ **Muslim**
   eats no shellfish
   only eats 'halal' meat
   drinks no alcohol
   fasts on a regular basis

Nice & Easy Does It!

♥ Cooking is supposed to give you pleasure so, don't let that dinner date cause you any stress.

♥ Luckily, modern thinking, technology and techniques have presented us with much easier ways of preparing for occasions quickly.

♥ So... cheat!, Buy that no anxiety ready-made pastry, caviar and ciabatta. Shortcuts? Maybe!

♥ But... if you're feeling adventurous, experiment. Add a bit of this and a bit of that and, more importantly, practise before the date!

♥ Don't forget weights, measures and temperatures, double-check!

♥ Also... consider appetite size and double-up the ingredients if necessary (excess food can be frozen).

♥ Bring out those creative talents of yours! Play with food presentation, make it funny, make it pretty or even appealingly sexy.

Anytime you like

Morning, noon or nightime...

There's no law that says romantic meals for two can only be eaten at night. Illuminating sunlight can be just as romantic as dusky moonlight.

In fact, anytime is the right time for romance! An intimate Breakfast, shared with a close companion, can give you the perfect start to the day.

A cosy Lunch 'a deux' can turn an ordinary day into a special occasion.

Enjoy a light, appetizing daytime meal with the object of your affections, and make hay while the sun shines!

Breakfast 1

FOREPLAY

Fresh Orange Juice

THE MAIN EVENT

Scrambled Eggs with
Smoked Salmon
served on Toasted
Bread Triangles

AFTERGLOW

Herbal Tea/Coffee/Tea

Scrambled Eggs with Smoked Salmon

Add a touch of colour to a common dish for a rare breakfast treat

4 eggs
45g (1½ oz) smoked salmon, flaked
coarse ground black pepper
sliced wholemeal bread

30 ml (1 oz) milk
salt
knob of butter

1. Beat the eggs gently and add the milk, salt and pepper.
2. Add the flaked fish.
3. Melt the butter in a pan then pour in the mixture and stir gently with a wooden spoon until cooked but moist.
4. Toast the bread put the scrambled eggs on top and cut into triangles, then serve.

TITBIT... Take it easy!

♥ For the best results when making love, a generous helping of relaxation is a must!

♥ Low lighting, soft music and a romantic dinner can all play a part in creating a relaxed atmosphere for you and your chosen playmate. The contents of the meal may also help you to unwind.

♥ An intake of sugar, for example, increases the number of opiate receptors in the brain, producing a calming, mellowed effect (similar to that produced by drugs like morphine and opium).

♥ Eggs and milk contain proteins that are especially rich in tryptophan. This amino acid encourages the production of a chemical called serotonin, which induces relaxation and is sometimes used in the making of antidepressant drugs.

♥ An added bonus is that these foods also provide nutrients that help to produce the body's energy.

♥ So, they can loosen you up and keep you going!

Breakfast 2

FOREPLAY

Pink Grapefruit

THE MAIN EVENT

'Smoky'
Croissants
Wholemeal buttered
bread triangles

AFTERGLOW

Herbal Tea/Coffee/Tea

(See photograph on pages 42-43)

'Smoky'

A smoky tit-bit to eat with your fingers, a subtle combination of smoked oysters and bacon for before or after.

8 slices rindless streaky bacon
8 smoked oysters
I lemon

1. Stretch the bacon with a knife and roll the oysters up in the bacon strips. Hold the rolls in place with cocktail sticks.
2. Place the bacon and oyster rolls on a tray and grill both sides for a few minutes until cooked.
3. Remove them from the grill, sprinkle them with lemon juice and serve with buttered wholemeal bread triangles.

Lunch 1

THE MAIN EVENT

Summer Whiting
Potato & Chilli Salad
Dressed Green Salad

AFTERGLOW

Adam & Eve

Dressed Green Salad

75g (2½ oz) frozen peas
½ Webb lettuce, washed and shredded
½ Cos lettuce, washed and shredded
½ cucumber, washed and sliced
2 salad spring onions, washed and cut into thin strips
2 tbsp olive oil
I tbsp white wine vinegar
I garlic clove, peeled and diced
¼ tsp celery seeds
lemon juice
salt

1. Put the peas into a bowl, cover them with boiling water and leave them to stand for 5 minutes.
2. Place the lettuce, cucumber, spring onions and peas in a salad bowl, then put the oil, vinegar, garlic, celery seeds, lemon juice and salt into a small bowl, mix well and pour over the salad. Toss and serve.

Summer Whiting

Fillets of white fish dressed in a light summer coat.

2 skinless whiting fillets
salt
pepper
plain flour
cooking oil
lemon wedges
fresh tarragon

1. Wash the fish, towel pat dry and sprinkle with salt and pepper to taste.
2. Heat the cooking oil in a frying pan until hot.
3. Sprinkle flour onto a clean surface and flour both sides of the fish then fry for 3-5 minutes each side until cooked through and golden brown.

4. Remove the fish from the pan and drain onto kitchen roll. Garnish with lemon wedges and fresh tarragon.

Serve hot or cold.

Potato & Chilli Salad

A 'Hot' potato salad in a soothing olive oil and mayonnaise dressing

2 large potatoes, peeled, washed and cubed
I small can sweetcorn
I fresh chilli pepper, chopped
3 tbsp mayonnaise
salt
I tbsp olive oil

1. Put the potato cubes into a pan of water and simmer them gently until they are cooked but still firm.
2. Strain and place the potatoes in a bowl then set them aside to cool.
3. When cooled, sprinkle them with salt, add the remaining ingredients and gently mix them together.
4. Refrigerate and serve chilled.

'Adam & Eve'

An irresistable dessert of forbidden fruit.

2 ripe bananas
2 eating apples
185g (6 oz) sugar
185 ml (6 fl oz) water
½ cinnamon stick

1. Put the sugar, cinnamon stick and water in a saucepan, bring to the boil and allow to boil for 10 minutes to form a syrup. Remove the cinnamon stick.

2. Meanwhile, wash and slice the apples ($\frac{1}{2}$ inch thick) and place them in a dish, flat sides down.

3. Slice the bananas down the middle and place the slices flat side down either side of the apple slices, then cover them with syrup.

4. Place them under a pre-heated grill and grill them on a low heat for 5-10 minutes until the apples are soft and the fruit brown on top.

5. Pour single cream over the fruit and serve immediately.

Eat me! (Apple)

Touch me
You know you want to
Feel how smooth my skin is
Feel how firm I am
Crisp
Juicy
Sweet
I'm all these things... and more
Go on
Take a bite
Sink your teeth into me
And make my juices flow
What are you waiting for?
You know I'm good for you
Do it!
You know you want to
Eat me

Lunch 2

THE MAIN EVENT

Seafood Galore
None of Your Sauce (Sauce Chienne)
and Shrimp Sauce
Hot Brioche

AFTERGLOW

Russian Melon

(See photograph on pages 44-45)

Seafood Galore

An arena of seafood from the depths of the ocean, for those who love the rich salty taste of the sea.

24 mussels
12 king prawns
1 packet mixed lettuce leaves

100g (3 oz) crabmeat
8-12 oysters
watercress

Put the lettuce leaves onto a platter, wash and drain the seafood and arrange with the lettuce then sprinkle the watercress evenly over the arrangement.

Serve with 'None of Your Sauce' (Sauce Chienne) and 'Shrimp Sauce'.

'None of Your Sauce!' (Sauce Chienne)

A hot, fiery sauce from the French-Caribbean, the perfect compliment to seafood.

100 ml (4 oz) vegetable oil
50 ml (2 oz) vinegar
1 onion, chopped
1 small hot red pepper, seeded and chopped
1 small garlic clove, chopped
½ tsp dried thyme
½ tsp dried mixed herbs
salt
coarse ground black pepper

1. Put all the ingredients into a mixing bowl and mix well, then add salt and black pepper to taste.
2. Cover the bowl and place it in a refrigerator overnight, then transfer to a sauce bowl or jar.

Shrimp Sauce

Let's get saucy with this mix of chunky and creamy textures, a cheeky little number to serve with fish.

60g (2 oz) fresh shrimps, peeled	**30g (1 oz) butter**
1 tsp plain flour	**½ an onion, diced**
125 ml (4 fl oz) fish stock	**1 small clove garlic, diced**
80 ml (3 fl oz) double cream	**1 tsp lemon juice**
salt	**pepper**

1. Melt the butter in a saucepan and sauté the onions until soft.
2. Stir in the flour and garlic.
3. Stir in the stock gradually and bring to the boil, stirring constantly.
4. Remove from the heat and stir in the cream, bring to the boil, reduce the heat and simmer for 15 minutes.
5. Add the shrimps to the sauce, together with the lemon juice, stir well and simmer gently for a further 5 minutes. Season to taste.

Russian Melon

Cut that melon in half, add pear pieces, pour on the vodka and... party!!!

1 water (or other) melon, halved and seeded
100 ml (4 fl oz) vodka
3 firm pears, peeled and seeded

1. Scoop out the melon flesh and cut it into cubes making sure the half melon skin shells are left in tact.
2. Scoop the pears into ball shapes using a small scoop.
3. Put the melon cubes and pear balls into the shells of the melon skins then pour the vodka evenly over the fruit.

Refrigate and serve chilled.

Whatever turns you on!

The association of food with sexual desire is not unique to any region of the world, nor to any particular period in history. Here are just a few examples of popular beliefs held by different peoples in times past:

Tomatoes (also known as 'love apples' or 'pommes d'amour') were thought to be an extremely potent aphrodisiac by the Cromwellians. So concerned were they about the possible effects of this lustful fruit, they deliberately spread false rumours that tomatoes were poisonous, to put people off eating them.

Prunes were very popular in Elizabethan times, particularly amongst the clients of brothels. Henry VIII was also said to be a big fan of prunes (and his reputation speaks for itself!)

Onions were considered highly erotic in ancient Egypt where priests were forbidden to eat them, for fear of losing control.

Chocolate was definitely off the menu in 17th century France. Members of religious orders were barred from eating chocolate as it would undoubtedly arouse inappropriate stirrings, leading to an inevitable fall from grace!

Apples were popular aphrodisiacs in medieval Germany. But, for maximum effect, they had to be soaked in the sweat of the desired person. This, it was believed, would provide the ultimate rush of sexual energy, making the aspiring lover uncontrollably horny!

Part 2

Making her way towards the check-out, she stopped to pick up the last remaining item on her shopping list. As she scanned the rows of products in the pharmacy section, she became aware of someone standing behind her.

"Excuse me," he said, leaning forward to retrieve something from the shelf in front of her. Without turning around, she moved slightly to one side. A strong, male hand reached over her shoulder, and removed a packet of condoms from the well-stocked display.

He was so close, she could smell him. A shiver of excitement rippled through her as his scent wafted around her. Drawn like a magnet, she turned and watched as he paid for his purchase and walked out of the store.

Hold the meat!

It is a fact of life that some people don't eat meat!

Serving it up in enticing and provocative ways won't tempt a vegetarian to eat the most sumptuous of meaty meals. So, given that romance doesn't have to go out the window along with the pork chops, here's a selection of menus suitable for those of vegetarian persuasion.

After all, vegetarians need love too!

Vegetarian 1

FOREPLAY

Pakora

THE MAIN EVENT

Puri
Channa (Chick Peas)
Spinach Bhaji

AFTERGLOW

Kulfi
Lassi

Pakora

Vegetables coated in seasoned wheat flour then fried until crispy.

1 aubergine (egg plant), washed and sliced
3 carrots, peeled and sliced
2 potatoes, peeled, washed and sliced like chips
breadcrumbs
½ tsp haldi (turmeric)
½ tsp ground chilli pepper
1 garlic clove, diced
1 egg, beaten
vegetable oil
pinch of salt

1. Put the bread crumbs, garlic, chilli pepper, haldi (turmeric) and salt into a mixing bowl and mix them together.
2. Pour the oil into a frying pan, (enough to deep fry the sliced vegetables) and heat until hot.
3. Dip the vegetable slices into the egg, shaking off any excess then, cover with breadcrumbs and fry, reducing the heat if necessary until cooked with a crisp, golden coating.

Serve hot.

Puri

Savoury fried 'cakes' to eat with meat, fish or vegetable dishes.

90g (3 oz) brown wheat (aata)
90g (3 oz) white flour
pinch of salt
cooking oil

1. Sieve the flour, wheat and salt into a bowl, add enough water to knead into a moist dough (a little at a time) then cover the dough with a clean, wet towel to keep it moist.

2. After preparing the Channa and the Spinach Bhaji, roll the dough into small balls, using the palms of your hand, then flatten them and using a rolling pin, roll them into circles.

4. Heat the oil in a frying pan until very hot and fry the puri for a few minutes each side until cooked.

Serve hot.

Channa

An abundance of spices adds aromatic piquancy to this pulse dish.

420g (13 oz) can cooked chick peas
2-3 garlic cloves, crushed
1 small onion, sliced
½ tsp cumin seeds
½ inch root ginger, crushed
2 tbsp oil
¼ tsp haldi (turmeric)
½ tsp ground chilli pepper
1 lemon, juiced
coriander leaves for garnishing
salt

1. Heat the oil in a pan then fry the onions and cumin seeds gently for 1 minute.
2. Add the haldi (turmeric) and red chilli pepper then mix until the mixture forms a curry paste.
3. Add the crushed ginger and garlic to the mixture and fry for another minute.
4. Add the chick peas and salt to taste, mix together and allow to warm through for 1 minute then remove from the heat.
5. Pour the lemon juice over the mixture, garnish with coriander leaves and serve.

Fresh chick peas can be used for this recipe but have to be soaked in water overnight and boiled for at least 1 hour until tender.

Spinach Bhaji

Spinach + spices = a knockout!

750g (1½ lbs) fresh spinach, washed and cut
2 or 3 garlic cloves, diced
1 small onion, cut into wedges
1 red capsicum, seeded and chopped
1 fresh chilli, seeded and chopped
1-2 tbsp cooking oil

1. Immerse the cut spinach in boiling water for 1 minute then, using a sieve or colander, drain off the water and set the spinach aside.
2. Pour the cooking oil into a pan, heat it until hot and fry the garlic and chopped peppers for a couple of minutes.
3. Add the spinach and fry for 1 more minute turning the vegetables constantly.

Remove from the heat and serve immediately or keep warm until ready to serve.

Kulfi

Cool and creamy with the icy crunch of almonds and pistachios

450 ml (16 fl oz) milk
20g (¾ oz) rice flour
150 ml (5 fl oz) evaporated milk
50g (2 oz) sugar
½ tbsp chopped almonds
½ tbsp chopped pistachios

1. Boil the milk in a saucepan then simmer until reduced to one third of the original quantity.
2. Gradually add the rice flour to the milk, stirring well.
3. Pour in the evaporated milk and continue to stir.

4. Lower the heat and simmer for 10-15 minutes then add the sugar and stir well until it dissolves.

5. Set aside to cool and then stir in half the pistachios and almonds.

6. Transfer the mixture to a freezable container and freeze until icy but not solid.

6. Remove the container from the freezer and beat the mixture until the ice melts, then return the kulfi to the freezer and freeze until firm.

Scoop into serving bowls, sprinkle with the remainder of the nuts and serve.

Lassi

An undressed beverage, best served ice cold.

> **600 ml (20 fl oz) milk**
> **600 ml (20 fl oz) natural yoghurt**
> **sugar to taste**

1. Put the yoghurt into a blender or jug, add the milk and the sugar to taste then blend until thick and frothy. To thin, if you prefer, add a little water.

2. Pour into tall glasses and serve.

A savoury Lassi can also be made by substituting the sugar for salt and pepper.

'No meat, please, we're vegetarian!'

The stereotypical image of the average vegetarian is that of a muscle-free weakling, lacking the strength and vigour of the mighty meat-eater!

If this is your view, it may interest you to know that vegetables feature prominently in the 'who's who' of aphrodisiacs.

When potatoes were first introduced into English society they were thought to be highly erotic sexual stimulants.

Carrots, tomatoes and celery have all enjoyed celebrity as inducers of uncontrollable lust. So have sweet potatoes, mushrooms, asparagus and onions (to name but a few).

Vegetables also provide a wide range of essential nutrients that help keep the body fit and healthy.

So, if you don't like eating vegetables, but you want to feel the benefit of them, a lusty vegetarian lover might be a tasty alternative!!

Vegetarian 2

FOREPLAY

Spicy Tomato & Pumpkin Soup

THE MAIN EVENT

Aubergines & Pasta
Ciabatta
Green Leaf & Herb Salad

AFTERGLOW

'Monkey-business'

(See photographs on pages 46-47 & 48)

Spicy Tomato & Pumpkin Soup

Ignite a flame with this spicy soup starter.

250g (8 oz) ripe tomatoes
75g (2½ oz) pumpkin, peeled, seeded and diced
½ an onion, diced
220 ml (7 fl oz) water
½ a vegetable stock cube
I tbsp butter
I tbsp plain flour
½ tsp basil
Tabasco sauce
chopped parsley

I. Cut the tomatoes into segments and strain them to remove the seeds, then set the juice aside.

2. Boil the pumpkin in a small amount of water until soft, then crush with a fork.

3. Melt the butter in a saucepan and gently fry the onion.

4. Lower the heat and stir in the flour and basil.

5. Add the tomato juice and water and bring to the boil, stirring constantly.

6. Crumble the vegetable cube into the liquid and stir. Cover and simmer for 15 minutes.

7. Strain the soup into another saucepan, sprinkle tabasco sauce to taste, stir well and reheat.

8. To serve divide the soup between two soup bowls. If liked, add one teaspoon of fresh cream, garnish with chopped parsley.

Aubergines with Pasta

A colourful concoction of egg plant and pasta, baked and topped with melted cheese.

- **2 medium aubergines, sliced**
- **1 large red pepper, seeded and sliced**
- **1 large green pepper, seeded and sliced**
- **2 garlic cloves, diced**
- **5 tomatoes, skinned, seeded and chopped**
- **2 tsp tomato puree**
- **6 tbsp red wine**
- **2 tbsp olive oil**
- **250g (8 oz) spinach tagliatelle, freshly cooked**
- **grated cheddar cheese**

1. Pour the olive oil into a saucepan and sauté the onions until soft.
2. Add the garlic, aubergines, tomatoes, green and red peppers, mix them together, cover and allow them to cook for 5 minutes.
3. Add the tomato puree, salt, pepper and red wine, then simmer for 10 minutes.
4. Remove from the heat, stir in the noodles, then pour the mixture into an oven dish and sprinkle the cheese evenly on top.
5. Bake in a preheated oven 190 C / 375 F / Gas Mark 5 for 15-20 minutes until golden brown on top.

Serve with warm Ciabatta (Italian bread) or baguettes and Green Leaf & Herb Salad.

Green Leaf & Herb Salad

A basic salad with a subtle hint of sage. Simple yet effective.

- **1 packet mixed lettuce leaves or a selection of your choice, washed and dried**
- **½ a cucumber, washed**
- **2 celery stalks**
- **two generous handfuls of watercress**
- **2 tbsp white wine vinegar**
- **3 tbsp olive oil**
- **1 tbsp fresh sage, chopped**
- **salt and black pepper**

1. Place the mixed lettuce leaves in a colander or sieve and wash them thoroughly under running cold water, then place them in a salad bowl.
2. Halve the cucumber lengthwise, then slice it thinly.
3. Wash the watercress, add it to the mixed lettuce leaves together with the half cucumber slices and toss them together.
3. Put the white wine vinegar into a bowl and add the olive oil, chopped sage, salt and black pepper to taste, mix well, spoon into the salad bowl and serve.

'Monkey-Business'

Banana fritters doused in rum sauce. Mmmm!!

I ripe banana
100g (3½ oz) self-raising flour
90 ml (3 fl oz) milk
I level tbsp brown sugar
pinch ground nutmeg
pinch ground cinnamon
pinch salt
cooking oil

1. Peel the banana, place it in a bowl and mash it with a fork.
2. Add the nutmeg, cinnamon, sugar, salt and milk and blend until smooth.
3. Sieve the flour and fold it into the mixture stirring well.
4. Heat the oil in a frying pan.
5. Dip a tablespoon into the hot oil to avoid sticking and dip it into the mixture.
6. Drop large spoonfuls of the mixture into the hot oil in circular shapes until all the mixture is used up.
6. Cook on moderate heat for 5 minutes either side until golden brown.
7. Place each fritter onto kitchen roll to remove the excess oil.
8. To keep them warm until ready to serve, place them on a dish over a pan of boiling water and cover.
9. Transfer to serving plates and pour the Rum Sauce over the hot fritters.

Serve immediately with ice cream or fresh, whipped cream.

Rum Sauce

60g (2 fl oz) sugar
100 ml (4 fl oz) cup water
100 ml (4 fl oz) cup rum

1. Mix together in a saucepan the sugar, water and rum.
2. Bring to the boil, stirring constantly until the sauce thickens.
3. Pour the sauce over the fritters and serve immediately.

Honey

Sticky fingers
Sticky fingers
Where have you been?
Dipping in and out
Of the honey pot
No doubt!

Pommes d'Amour
(Tomatoes)

I'd been seeing this guy for ages
And my love for him was real
So I thought I'd have him over
And cook us both a meal
I wanted to feed him something
That would stoke his smouldering ember
Like oysters (but they cost a bomb!)
When, suddenly, I remember
My mate (a chef) advised me
To give him 'pommes d'amour'
"It'll put lead in his pencil!
It says so in folklore."
So I bought two huge tomatoes
(And some other things I'd need)
Split them in the middle
And dug out all the seed
Then I cooked some rice, with prawns and herbs
And stuffed it all inside
Baked for twenty minutes
And served it up with pride
He devoured that meal ravenously...
I followed close behind!
He couldn't get enough of me
But I really didn't mind
I'll miss out all the juicy bits
Suffice it just to say
That guy is now my husband
We got married yesterday
So, if you want to get your man
Just feed him 'pommes d'amour'
And before the night is over
He'll be whispering "Je t'adour!"

Vegetarian 3 ♥

FOREPLAY

Chilli Plantain Crisps
Guacamole

THE MAIN EVENT

Braised Okra
Boiled Green Bananas
Jollof Rice

AFTERGLOW

Kiwi Water Ice

♥ suitable for vegans

Chilli Plantain Crisps

These tropical titbits are hotter than they sound!

2 green plaintains, skinned   **ground chilli pepper**
cooking oil   **salt**

1. Slice the plantains into thin round crisp-shaped pieces, place them in a bowl of water for 15 minutes, then drain off the water.
2. Dry the pieces with a clean towel and sprinkle them evenly with chilli pepper and salt.
3. Heat enough oil in a pan to deep-fry the plantain pieces, then fry them until crispy and golden brown.

Serve with Guacamole.

Guacamole

A popular Mexican dip, made with smooth avocados, seasoned and combined with sour cream.

2 large avocados, stoned   **2 tbsp vegetable oil**
1 onion, chopped   **2 garlic cloves, diced**
150 ml (5 fl oz) sour cream/natural soya yoghurt
½ tsp ground chilli pepper   **3 large tomatoes, skinned**
4 tsp lemon juice   **ground black pepper**
salt

1. Heat the oil in a pan and add the onions, garlic and chilli pepper, fry until the onions are soft then chop the skinned tomatoes, add to the mixture and fry for a further 5 minutes until the tomatoes are mashed.
2. Pour the mixture into a blender and blend until smooth then, pour into a bowl and set aside to cool.
3. Scoop the flesh from the avocados and add it to the bowl, then add the lemon juice and mix well until smooth.
4. Blend in the sour cream, transfer the mixture to a serving dish.
5. To serve, garnish with salad and sprinkle lightly with chilli pepper.

Photographs of the menus below are shown in the following pages:

BREAKFAST 2 (from page 15)
Pink Grapefruit, 'Smoky', Croissants, Herbal Tea & Orange Juice

LUNCH 2 (from page 21)
Seafood Galore with Shrimp Sauce & Sauce Chienne & Hot Brioche,
Melon with Pears in Vodka

VEGETARIAN 2 (from page 33)
Spicy Tomato & Pumpkin Soup, Aubergines & Pasta, Greenleaf &
Herb Salad

VEGETARIAN DESSERT
'Monkey Business'

Braised Okra

Fiery okra, commonly known as 'lady's fingers', prepared in a traditionally Asian style and cooked in creamy coconut milk.

25g (1 oz) ghee
½ large onion, sliced
2 garlic cloves, crushed
½ inch fresh ginger, peeled and chopped
1 green chilli, chopped
¼ tsp ground chilli pepper
225g (8 oz) okra
125 ml (4 fl oz) water
salt
1 tbsp coconut milk

1. Melt the ghee in a heavy pan, add the onion, garlic, ginger, chopped chilli and chilli pepper.
2. Fry gently for 5 minutes until soft, stirring occasionally.
3. Top and tail the okras, wash and add them to the mixture.
4. Add the water and salt to taste.
5. Bring to the boil then lower the heat, cover and simmer for 5 minutes until the okras are tender.
6. Stir in the coconut milk and serve hot.

As well as making an excellent vegetarian main course, this dish may be served as an accompaniment.

Boiled Green Bananas

4 green bananas
1.5 litres (45 fl oz) water
salt
knob of butter (optional)

1. Pour the water into a saucepan, add the salt and bring to the boil.

2. Wash the bananas, cut off their tops and tails and slice their skins downwards.

3. Place the bananas in boiling water and allow them to boil in their skins for 20-30 minutes until tender (test by pushing the sharp end of a knife through the skin).

4. When cooked, remove the bananas from their skins and slice.

5. Place on a serving dish with a knob of butter and serve hot immediately.

Jollof Rice

A Nigerian style rice dish, hotly spiced with fresh hot peppers, garlic and onions and steamed until light and fluffly.!

315g (11oz) rice
2 tbsp tomato puree
½ an onion, chopped
¼ hot fresh pepper, seeded and diced
1 garlic clove, diced
1 tbsp cooking oil
salt
500 ml (16 fl oz) water

1. Pour the cooking oil into a saucepan, add the garlic, hot pepper and onions, then sauté until soft.

2. Add the tomato puree, salt to taste and mix everything together.

3. Pour the water into the mixture and bring to the boil.

4. Add the rice, stir, cover and reduce the heat.

5. Allow the jollof rice to steam cook until light and fluffy, adding small amounts of boiling water if neccesary.

Serve hot.

Kiwi Water Ice

4-6 kiwi fruit, skinned
90g (3½ oz) granulated sugar
75 ml (2½ fl oz) water
lemon juice

1. Place the sugar and water in a saucepan, heat slowly until the sugar is dissolved, then boil for 2 minutes until the mixture thickens to a syrup. Remove from the heat and set aside to cool.
2. Cut the kiwi fruit into wedges, place them in a saucepan, add 1 tablespoon of water to the pan, cover and allow to simmer gently for 2 minutes.
3. Remove the pan from the heat, blend the kiwi fruit mixture until smooth then stir in the cool syrup, add a little lemon juice and mix well.
4. Pour the fruit mixture into a freezable container and freeze for 1 hour.
5. After 1 hour remove the partly frozen mixture from the freezer, beat well to remove the icy crystals.
6. Return the mixture to the freezer and repeat this process every hour until the ice is set and ready to serve. (The process takes approximately 3-4 hours).

Serve in chilled glasses, garnished with mint leaves.

Firing on all cylinders!

All kinds of different food items are credited with having aphrodisiac properties (even foods that do not have an obviously 'sexy' image). However, a closer look at the nutritional make-up of these foods may explain how they came by their lusty reputation.

The human body is made up of a complex network of materials which keep all it's parts in good running order. Vitamins and minerals provide the nutrients needed to keep the body oiled, tuned and in peak condition. Most of these substances are obtained from what we eat, and it is foods that provide this essential nourishment that are commonly labelled 'aphrodisiac'.

For example, asparagus, peanuts and mushrooms are rich in folic acid; an important ingredient in the production of histamine. Histamine (or the lack of it) is thought to affect the ability of men and women to reach orgasm when having sex.

Hardly surprising, then, that these foods are all reputed aphrodisiacs.

Vegetarian 4 ♥

FOREPLAY

Bean Salad

THE MAIN EVENT

Three Pepper Curry
Saffron & Almond Rice
Raita (Cucumber & Yoghurt)
Green Mint Salad

AFTERGLOW

Gingered Peaches

♥ suitable for vegans

(See photograph on pages 82-83)

Bean Salad

A lively salad, full of beans!

125g (4 oz) kidney beans
I large potato, peeled and cubed
I onion
¼ sweet pepper, seeded and thinly sliced
pepper
salt
I tbsp mixed herbs
I tbsp wine vinegar
½ tsp mustard
½ tsp sugar
3 tbsp olive oil

1. Soak the beans overnight in cold water.
2. Boil the beans with the onions and garlic until they are cooked but firm. Add salt to taste, drain and set aside in a bowl.
3. Place the potato cubes in enough boiling water to cover them and boil for a few minutes until cooked but firm. Drain and set them aside to cool.
4. Add the sweet peppers, mixed herbs and black pepper to the beans, then add the cooled potato cubes and mix them together.
5. Mix together the vinegar, sugar, mustard and oil, whisk them well, then pour the mixture over the beans.

Serve chilled.

Three Pepper Curry

A vibrant mosaic of red, gold and green peppers in a spicy curry sauce.

I large yellow pepper seeded and cut into chunks
I large red pepper seeded and cut into chunks
I large green pepper seeded and cut into chunks
I large onion, chopped

- **1 garlic clove, diced**
- **1 red chilli pepper, seeded and chopped**
- **2 tbsp vegetable oil**
- **½ tsp turmeric**
- **½ inch fresh root ginger, peeled and crushed**
- **300 ml (10 fl oz) vegetable stock**

1. Put the vegetable oil into a saucepan, heat and add the sliced onions then add the garlic, red chilli pepper, ginger and turmeric. Fry gently stirring continuously until the mixture becomes a paste.
2. Continue to stir whilst slowly adding the vegetable stock, then add the chunks of sweet peppers and bring to the boil.
3. Reduce the heat, cover the pan and allow to it simmer for 5-10 minutes until the peppers are cooked but firm. Transfer to a serving dish and serve hot.

Saffron & Almond Rice

Golden rice with an almond surprise.

- **75g (2½ oz) ghee**
- **1 onion, sliced**
- **15g (½ oz) almonds, chopped**
- **220g (7 oz) rice**
- **375 ml (13 fl oz) boiling water**
- **¼ tsp ground saffron**
- **½ tsp whole cloves**
- **2 whole cardamoms**
- **½ tsp salt**
- **parsley**

1. Melt the ghee in a saucepan, add the onions and fry until soft.
2. Using a sieve, wash the rice through with cold water, drain well and add to the onions, then add the seasonings and spice and stir-fry for 3 minutes.
3. Add the saffron and stir well, then pour the boiling water into the saucepan and bring to the boil. Lower the heat and simmer for 15 minutes until the rice is cooked.

4. Whilst the rice is cooking, heat a frying pan and dry roast the chopped almonds and then set them aside.

5. Drain the rice and spoon it into a serving bowl, add the dry roasted almonds and stir. Garnish with parsley and serve hot.

Raita

Keep your cool with this cucumber and yoghurt relish.

> **150 ml (5 fl oz) natural yoghurt or soya yoghurt**
> **½ cucumber, diced or cut into short strips**
> **½ small onion, chopped**
> **¼ tsp ground chilli pepper**
> **¼ tsp fresh chopped coriander**
> **salt**

1. Put the yoghurt, cucumber and onions in a mixing bowl and stir well.

2. Spoon the Raita into a serving dish, sprinkle with coriander leaves and chilli pepper.

3. Place in the refrigerator and serve chilled.

Green Mint Salad

> **I small cucumber**
> **½ a lettuce**
> **2 sprigs fresh mint, chopped**
> **3 tbsp olive oil**
> **juice of I lime**
> **2 tbsp white vinegar**
> **pinch of salt**

1. Wash and chop the cucumber into cubes

2. Wash and shred the lettuce.

3. Place the lettuce and cucumber in a bowl.

4. Put the olive oil, juice of the lime, vinegar and salt into a small bowl and whisk.

5. Add the chopped mint to the mixture, pour evenly over the salad and serve.

Gingered Peaches

A decadent dessert to enflame and consume.

30g (1 oz) crystallised ginger, diced
30g (1 oz) butter
1 small can halved peaches
1 tbsp soft brown sugar
1 tbsp brandy

1. Drain the peaches well and set them aside, then melt the butter in a saucepan. Add the sugar and the ginger and stir until the sugar dissolves into the butter.
2. Add the peaches to the butter mixture and sauté gently until the fruit is warm.
3. Place the peaches onto a warm serving dish, gently warm the brandy and pour it over the peaches, then set them alight. Garnish with brandy snaps and serve.

Fresh peaches can be used in this recipe, simply stone, skin and halve them, then sauté them for a little longer than the canned peaches until tender and warm.

Up... up... and away!

Drugs can give you a high. Love can give you a high. Sex can give you a high. But did you know about bananas?

The common or garden banana isn't just a source of dietary fibre (and a source of endless fun for people of lewd inclination!) The skin of this rather erotically shaped fruit is, apparently, full of an hallucinogen called bufotenine. (Hence warnings about 'tripping' on banana skins?!)

As mind-altering drugs can stimulate sexual fantasy, this could account for the aphrodisiac reputation of bananas.

Interestingly, bufotenine is also found on the skin of toads. This puts a whole new slant on the romantic tale of the maiden who kissed a toad and saw it turn into a prince. One has to wonder, did the toad really turn into a prince... or was the maiden stoned?

Part 3

She usually paid close attention to the prices being rung up on the cash register. But not today. Instead, she stared idly through the window, watching as he strolled leisurely towards his parked car. He moved with the assurance of a man who was comfortable inside his own body, exuded an air of blatant sexuality, suggestive of a confident lover.

Aroused by the lingering scent of him, she started to undress him in her mind, peeling off each layer of clothing, until he stood naked before her. Her eyes travelled slowly over his nude body, taking in every inch of his manliness.

The vividness of the image excited her. She longed to touch him; to taste him; to hear his sighs as he succumbed to the pleasure of her caresses.

Totally caught up in the fantasy, she felt his heart beat next to hers as they lay together gently moving in time to their own intimate rhythm, taking each other to the edge of heaven... and beyond!

UP . . .

With the onset of Spring comes a universal thaw, as temperatures start to rise. This is the season in which things generally begin to stir. Trees blossom. Flowers burst into bloom. Creatures rise from their winter beds. And 'amour' stirs in the hearts (and loins) of human beings.

Summer sees passions rise and temperatures peak. It's a time for sun, sea, sand, beachwear and barbecues. And a perfect time to indulge in fine dining, al fresco, with an intimate friend.

Rise to any occasion with mouth-watering meals, ideal for the warm spring and summer months.

♥

Spring I

FOREPLAY

Prawns & Avocado

THE MAIN EVENT

Lamb with Rosemary
Roast Potatoes
Broccoli & Carrots
in Parsley Sauce

AFTERGLOW

Champagne Sorbet

(See photographs on pages 86-87 & 88)

Prawns & Avocado

Old faithful... but still a favourite.

1 large avocado	30g (1oz) peeled prawns
1 tbsp vinegar	1 tbsp olive oil
½ tsp chopped parsley	1 tsp lemon juice
pinch of salt	pinch of white pepper

1. Cut the avocado in two and remove the stone, then carefully scoop out the flesh from each half, without damaging the skin.
2. Put the flesh into a bowl and crush with a fork until soft and creamy.
3. Add the prawns, vinegar, olive oil, lemon juice, salt and pepper to taste and stir gently until combined.
4. Spoon the mixture into each case, sprinkle with chopped parsley and serve.

Lamb with Rosemary

Tender roast lamb with the bitter-sweet flavour of rosemary.

750g (1½ lb) top or half top leg of lamb
gravy granules
water
knob of butter
salt and black pepper

1. Place the leg of lamb into a roasting tin, sprinkle the chopped rosemary over the lamb, then put the knob of butter on top and cover with baking foil.
2. Pre-heat the oven to 350 F / 180 C / Gas Mark 4, put the lamb in the oven and roast for 80 minutes.
3. Remove the foil and roast for a further 20 minutes, basting occasionally. Using a sharp slim knife, pierce through the meat and if the juices are clear, remove the lamb from the oven and place it onto a chopping board or clean surface and leave it to rest for 10 or so minutes before carving.

up

4. Meanwhile, to make the gravy, place the roasting tin on a low heat and top up the meat juices with water then add the gravy granules to the liquid. Stir well with a wooden spoon until the granules dissolve and bring to the boil.
5. Reduce the heat, transfer the gravy to a saucepan and allow to simmer for 5 minutes until thick and creamy.
6. Slice the lamb thinly and serve with vegetables, and lots of gravy.

Roast Potatoes

You can't beat them!!

500g (1 lb) potatoes, peeled and washed
2 tbsp cooking oil

1. Par-boil the potatoes in a salted water, remove and strain.
2. Pre-heat the oven to 375 F / 190 C / Gas Mark 5 then put the cooking oil into a clean, dry roasting tin and place it in the oven to heat for five minutes.
3. Carefully put the potatoes into the hot oil and turn them with a wooden spoon until they are all basted with hot oil then allow them to roast until crisp and golden (about 45 minutes to 1 hour).
4. Serve immediately with roast meat and vegetables.

Broccoli & Carrots in Parsley Sauce

Make plain vegetables more appealing with seductive pour-over sauces.

250 g (8 oz) baby carrots
250 g (8 oz) broccoli

1. Place the vegetables into a saucepan then mix 6 tablespoons of water with a pinch of salt and 1/4 teaspoon of sugar until dissolved and pour the liquid over the vegetables. Allow them to steam for 10-15 minutes on a low heat.

2. Strain the vegetables using a colander or sieve, then cover them with the parsley sauce.

To make the sauce:

30g (1 oz) butter   **30g (1oz) flour**
500 ml (17 fl oz) milk   **1 tbsp chopped parsley**
salt and pepper

1. Melt the butter in a pan on a low heat, then add the flour and stir well until cooked dry.
2. Set the saucepan aside and add the milk slowly, little by little, stirring constantly to blend out the lumps.
3. Return the saucepan to the fire and bring to boil, stirring constantly. Add the parsley and boil for a further 5 minutes.
4. Add salt and pepper to taste then pour the sauce over the vegetables and serve immediately.

Champagne Sorbet

Complement a perfect meal with something expensive and heady!

125 ml (4 fl oz) champagne   **45g (1½ oz) granulated sugar**
1 small orange   **3 tbsp water**
fresh whole mint leaves

1. Peel the orange, squeeze the juice and grate half of the rind.
2. Put the water, sugar and grated rind into a pan and heat until the sugar dissolves, then set it aside to cool.
3. Strain the liquid and pour it into a bowl, add the champagne and mix it together.
4. Put the mixture into a freezable container, freeze until icy (about 1 hour) then remove and beat out the ice crystals.
5. Refreeze and repeat, then leave for 2 hours until set.

Serve in scoops, plain or dressed with fresh mint leaves.

Spring 2

FOREPLAY

Mussel Soup

THE MAIN EVENT

Tagliatelle & Smoked Salmon
Sweet Pepper & Caper Salad

AFTERGLOW

Zabaglione

Mussel Soup

Fond of mussels? You'll love this!

1 quart live mussels
1 onion diced
1 clove garlic, diced
150 ml (5 fl oz) white wine
1oz butter
1 tbsp fresh chopped parsley
coarse ground black pepper
salt
juice of one lemon

1. Discard any broken mussels and scrub clean the remainder, then place them in a saucepan and add the onions, garlic, butter, wine and half the chopped parsley.

2. Cover the pan and cook on a high heat for 5-10 minutes, shaking the pan regularly. Remove the pan from the heat and discard any mussels that have remained closed.

3. Strain the liquid from the mussels, place the mussels in serving bowls and keep warm.

4. Pour the liquid back in the saucepan and add the black pepper and salt to taste, boil for 1 minute, strain, then divide the liquid evenly between the serving bowls with the mussels.

5. Sprinkle the remainder of the parsley over the soup, add a little lemon juice and serve immediately.

Tagliatelle & Smoked Salmon

When in doubt, choose pasta. It's loved by most, quick to prepare and very tasty.

250g (8 oz) plain and spinach tagliatelle
125g (4 oz) smoked salmon, sliced
30g (1 oz) mushrooms, sliced
1 tsp fresh chopped parsley

1 spring onion, chopped
1 tsp butter
1 garlic clove, diced
4 tbsp double cream
salt and pepper
1 egg

1. Place the pasta in a saucepan of lightly salted boiling water and cook until tender but not soggy. Strain in a sieve or colander and set aside.
2. Heat the butter gently in a pan and cook the sliced mushrooms, onions and garlic until soft.
3. Beat the egg with the cream, add salt and pepper to taste, then pour the mixture onto the mushrooms and onion, mix well and re-heat, stirring constantly.
4. Put the cooked pasta and strips of smoked salmon into a bowl, pour the creamy mixture on top and mix with a fork and spoon (toss as with salads).
5. Garnish with fresh parsley and serve.

Sweet Pepper & Caper Salad

½ red pepper, seeded
½ green pepper, seeded
½ yellow pepper, seeded
1 tbsp capers
½ tbsp white wine vinegar
1 garlic clove, diced
olive oil
salt and pepper

1. Using a sharp knife, slice the peppers into fairly thick strips and grill them under a preheated grill for 1 minute.
2. Remove the peppers from under the grill and place them in a serving dish. Sprinkle them with the garlic, black pepper, salt and capers.
3. Mix a tablespoon of olive oil with the white wine vinegar and pour evenly over the salad then chill in the refrigerator for 40 minutes.

Zabaglione

Tricky to make but beautiful to eat.

2 egg yolks   **45g (1½ oz) caster sugar**
60 ml (2 fl oz) Marsala (or substitute with any other dessert wine)

1. Put the egg yolks and sugar into a large heatproof bowl over a saucepan of simmering water and beat together until they form a pale, thick mixture.
2. Keep whisking for 15-20 minutes whilst gradually adding the Marsala until thick and frothy. (Always add the wine gradually to avoid separation of the mixture).
3. Pour into serving glasses and serve immediately.

TITBIT...

Winner takes all!

Staying power is an essential asset for any would-be sexual athlete. So, before you enter the sexual arena, you might want to top up your reserves of energy. Carbohydrates, fats and proteins are our main sources of energy which fuels the body, giving it stamina and power. Energy is also used to generate body heat. Aphrodisiac status has, thus, been enjoyed by many energy-giving foods, such as:

♥ **honey** (carbohydrate) – a libido booster favoured by the Romans
♥ **beans** (protein) – nuns were once instructed not to eat them for fear of being unfrocked!
♥ **cream** (fat) – which has probably starred in more sexual fantasies than you've had hot dinners!!

Alcohol, the favourite sexual stimulant of millions, is also a supplier of energy.

So, when preparing for a sexual marathon, remember: good technique alone may get you on the medals table, but an injection of energy could put you on course for gold!

Summer I

FOREPLAY

Chilled Avocado Soup

THE MAIN EVENT

Ginger Chicken Escalopes
Minty Taties
Red Cabbage and
Pickled Onion Salad

AFTERGLOW

Miel Strawberries & Cream

(See photograph on pages 84-85)

Chilled Avocado Soup

A wonderful summer soup made from avocado with the added 'zing' of spring onion and lime.

1 large avocado	the stalk of 1 spring onion, chopped
500 ml (1 pint) milk	1 tsp lime juice
salt	coarse ground black pepper
chopped parsley	

1. Scoop the flesh from the avocado and put into a blender
2. Add the other ingredients and blend for two minutes until smooth
3. Add salt and pepper to taste and serve.

Serve chilled garnished with chopped parsley

Ginger Chicken Escalopes

Do you like the taste of garlic? If so, this is for you... but don't forget your toothbrush!

2 large, skinned, boneless chicken breasts	
2 cloves garlic, diced	2 tbsp dried breadcrumbs
1 tsp dried thyme	coarse ground black pepper
1 inch root ginger, peeled and diced	salt
1 egg, beaten	cooking oil

1. Wash and towel pat dry the chicken breasts retaining some moisture and then flatten with a mallet.
2. Sprinkle the chicken breasts with, black pepper, salt and thyme.
3. Firmly press the diced garlic and ginger evenly into the chicken breasts.
4. Set aside for 15 minutes.
5. Quickly dip the chicken into the beaten egg then remove and coat with breadcrumbs.
6. Heat the oil until moderately hot then fry the breaded chicken on

medium heat for 5 minutes on either side until cooked through.

Serve hot or cold.

Minty Taties

Understated chic!

> **280g (9 oz) new potatoes, scrub-washed**
> **1 tsp fresh spearmint, chopped**
> **30g (1 oz) butter**

1. Put the potatoes into a saucepan of boiling, salted water and allow them to boil for 15 minutes until tender.
2. Drain and place the cooked potatoes into an oven dish, add the butter and sprinkle with the mint, stir a little, cover and place in a pre-heated oven 180 C / 350 F / Gas Mark 4 for a further 10-15 minutes. Remove from the oven and serve hot.

Red Cabbage & Pickled Onion Salad

Tangy on the tongue.

> **350g (11 oz) red cabbage, washed and shredded**
> **3 medium pickled onions, sliced**
> **salt and black pepper**
> **parsley to garnish**

1. Put the cabbage in a bowl of water which has just boiled, cover and blanch for 3 minutes then drain and set aside.
2 Arrange the cooled cabbage in a dish, add the onion slices, then sprinkle with salt and pepper to taste. Toss, dress with a vinagrette or salad dressing of your choice, garnish with parsley and serve cold.

Miel Strawberries

Rolled in warm honey and smothered with whipped cream. What a way to go!

1 punnet fresh strawberries, washed and topped
clear honey (to taste)   **whipping cream**
ground cinnamon

1. Cut the washed strawberries and slit each one in half then divide between two serving bowls
2. Place a bowl over a saucepan of boiling water, add the honey and cinnamon, then stir while it heats gently.
3. Whip the cream.
4. Pour the warm cinnamon honey evenly over the strawberries and toss gently with a heated spoon.

Serve immediately with the whipped cream

Let's Chill (Ice-cream)

A long, hot day that doesn't seem to want to end
Limp hair clinging to the back of my neck
Moisture oozing from my every pore
Making me wet
A raging fire burns inside and out
Igniting my craving for you
You look so cool
I want you, and I want you now!
Naked and unadorned
No chocolate chips
No tutti frutti bits
Just come as you are
And let me plunge my tongue into your chilling mound
And lick you from my fingers
When you drip.

Summer 2

FOREPLAY

Prawns in Creole Sauce

THE MAIN EVENT

Full-bellied Trout
Buttered Vegetables

AFTERGLOW

Mango Mousse

Prawns in Creole Sauce

Mouth-watering parcels of prawns in a piquant sauce wrapped in crisp lettuce leaves.

155g (5 oz) cooked, peeled salad prawns
1 small crispy lettuce

juice of 1 lemon
cocktail sticks

For the Creole Sauce:

2 tbsp olive oil
1 onion, diced
1 large tomato, peeled and seeded (or 1 small can peeled tomatoes)
1 fresh hot pepper, seeded and diced
salt & fresh ground black pepper
1 tbsp vinegar

1. Heat the oil in a pan, add the onion then sauté until soft.
2. Add the tomatoes, hot pepper and salt and pepper to taste.
3. Stir in the vinegar and cook for 3 minutes then set aside to cool.
4. Place the prawns in a bowl and squeeze lemon juice over them.
5. Tear off whole lettuce leaves and wash them thoroughly, keeping them whole.
6. Pat them dry with a tea towel then spoon 1 tablespoon of prawns into each one and cover the prawns with 1 teaspoon of sauce.
7. Roll up each lettuce leaf into a parcel and secure by pushing a cocktail stick through.
8. Dress with vinaigrette and serve chilled.

Full-bellied Trout

Bursting with goodness this wholesome dish should satisfy the most ravenous appetite.

2 fresh rainbow trout, cleaned
1 large potato, peeled and diced
¼ tsp dried thyme

155 ml (5 fl oz) fish stock
½ onion, diced
1 tbsp crushed almonds

up ...

2 tbsp soy sauce	**coarse ground black pepper**
salt	**2 tbsp butter**

1. Put the diced potatoes in a bowl, cover with boiling, salted water and allow to blanch for 15 minutes then drain and set aside to cool.
2. Put the remainder of the ingredients into a bowl and mix them together, then add the cooled potatoes and stir well.
3. Using a spoon, fill the trout with the mixture but not to overflowing.
4. Place the fish in an oven dish and pour on the fish stock, then add a tablespoon of butter.
5. Place the dish in a preheated oven at 180 C / 350 F / Gas Mark 4 and cook for 25 minutes, basting with the juices to keep the fish moist.

Garnish and serve hot.

Buttered Vegetables

Long, slender stems of asparagus and thick carrot ribbons... dripping in melted butter.

12 asparagus tips
250g (8 oz) carrots, peeled, cut into long, thick strips
60g (2 oz) butter
90 ml (3 fl oz) water

1. Place the asparagus and carrots in a pan with the water and steam until cooked but still firm.
2. Remove the vegetables and place them in a dish.
3. Melt the butter, pour it over the vegetables and serve.

Mango Mousse

Melts in the mouth.

125g (4 oz) tinned mango slices
⅓ tbsp unflavoured gelatine (if preferred use pectin)

125 ml (4 fl oz) water
200 ml (6½ fl oz) double cream, whisked
I egg

1. Put the water and gelatin into blender or a mixing bowl and blend or mix until dissolved.
2. Add the mango slices and blend until smooth.
3. Add the double cream and blend.
4. Whisk the egg white and fold it into the mixture.
5. Pour into dessert glasses and place in the refrigerator until firmly set.

Keep refrigerated until ready to serve.

TITBIT...

Sounds fishy to me!

Seafood has long been associated with increased sexual drive; none more so than oysters.

The most notorious lust provoker of all, oysters contain high levels of phosphorus, from which the body derives energy.

More significantly, oysters boast a very high concentration of zinc; a mineral closely connected to sexual performance. (There is also a high concentration of zinc in male sperm!) Scientific studies have shown that zinc deficiency can result in male impotence and a lack of ovulation in women.

The legendary lover, Casanova, was said to eat as many as 50 oysters a day and his sexual prowess remains the envy of many a man!

A note of caution if you're considering increasing your zinc intake: an excess of zinc in the system can be harmful to the body.

Part 4

"I SAID, WILL THAT BE CASH OR CHEQUE?!!"
The question brought her back to reality
with a start!
"What...?! Oh... um... cheque," she stuttered,
conscious of the curious stares of her fellow
shoppers. A hot flush of embarrassment washed
over her as she realised she must have been
standing there for some time, oblivious
to her surroundings.

She quickly wrote out a cheque, and thrust it in
the direction of the cashier. Avoiding eye contact,
she accepted the receipt, gathered up her
shopping bags, and hurriedly left the store.
Outside, she took a deep breath of fresh air to
clear her head.

Before making her way across the forecourt, she
looked over to the spot where he had parked
his car. He was still sitting there, in the driver's seat.
A knowing smile spread across her face. He was
waiting for her...

...and down!

Cool Autumn (or 'Fall') heralds the coming of the winter chill. The desire to wrap up tight increases. Evenings spent in indoor comfort become more frequent. And thoughts turn to nesting.

The cold Winter nights could have been made for romance. What better way to spend an evening than relaxing in your own cosy nook, enjoying an exquisite meal with the person you'd most like to be kept warm by?

When temperatures drop, stoke the home fires with meals to warm body, heart and soul.

Autumn 1

FOREPLAY

Leeky Soup

THE MAIN EVENT

Steamy Bream
Boiled Dumplings & Yam
Callaloo

AFTERGLOW

Torte Italienne

(See photograph on pages 122-123)

Leeky Soup

You won't leave a drop!

1 leek, scrub-washed and sliced thinly	
15g (½ oz) butter	½ onion, chopped
15g (½ oz) plain flour	220 ml (7 fl oz) vegetable stock
chopped parsley	salt and black pepper

1. Melt the butter in a saucepan, add the chopped onions and sauté until soft.
2. Stir in the flour and cook for approximately 1/2 a minute then gradually add the stock, stirring constantly.
3. Bring to the boil, add the leeks, lower the heat and simmer for 10-15 minutes until the leeks are soft.
4. Remove the soup from the heat, add salt and pepper to taste, garnish with chopped parsley and serve hot.

Steamy Bream

Cooked in herbs and spices. Quite a catch!

1 large red bream, scaled & cleaned	1 onion, sliced
1 garlic clove, diced	1 large tomato, sliced
½ green pepper	4 sprigs fresh thyme
salt	coarse ground black pepper
2 tbsp cooking oil	1 tbsp butter

1. Place the fish in a large pan or fish steamer.
2. Sprinkle garlic, salt and pepper evenly over the fish.
3. Arrange the onions and tomatoes over the fish and top with the fresh thyme
4. Add cooking oil and butter to the pan, cover and allow to steam on a low heat for 20-30 minutes until tender and swimming in natural juices.

Serve immediately.

Photographs of the menus below are shown in the following pages:

VEGETARIAN 4 (from page 53)
Bean Salad, Three Pepper Curry, Saffron & Almond Rice, Raita, Green Mint Salad, Naan, Gingered Peaches

SUMMER 1 (from page 69)
Chilled Avocado Soup, Ginger Chicken Escalopes, Minty Taties, Red Cabbage & Pickled Onion Salad, Miel Strawberries & Cream

SPRING 1 (from page 61)
Prawns & Avocado, Lamb with Rosemary, Broccoli & Carrot in Parsley Sauce

SPRING DESSERT
Champagne Sorbet

Boiled Dumplings & Yams

Savour the blend of different textures in these tropical island favourites.

350g (11 oz) yam, peeled and thickly sliced
250g (8 oz) plain flour   **4 tbsp cornmeal**
½ tsp salt   **125 ml (4 fl oz) water**

1. Put a saucepan of salted, water to boil then sieve the flour, cornmeal and salt into a bowl and mix well together.
2. Using a pastry cutter, cut round shapes out of the sliced yam, put them into a bowl of cold water and set aside.
3. Gradually pour 125 ml (4 fl oz) cold water into the sieved flour mixture and stir it until it forms a stiff dough.
4. Sprinkle a little flour onto a clean surface and knead the dough.
5. Shape the dough into small balls and, using the thumb, press a small dent into each one.
6. Put the balls of dough into the boiling water, lower the heat to medium, allow to boil for 5 minutes, then add the round pieces of yam. Boil gently until the yam is cooked but firm and the dumplings are firm but not too solid.
7. Remove the yam and dumplings from the saucepan, drain and serve hot.

Callaloo

A leafy green vegetable with a flavour all its own.

500g (1 lb) callaloo, canned or fresh, trimmed and chopped
1 onion, sliced   **1 tomato, diced**
salt   **coarse ground black pepper**
cooking oil

1. Heat the cooking oil in a saucepan.
2. Add the onions, tomatoes, black pepper and salt, then sauté them for 1 minute.
3. Drain the callaloo into a sieve and add it to the pan, stir, cover and allow to simmer for 5 minutes.

4. Remove from the heat and serve hot.

Fresh Callaloo can also be used: wash well, thinly slice the stalks and cook for an extra eight minutes.

Torte Italienne

Be indulgent, with this fantastic Italian dessert – Amaretti cookies, mascarpone cheese, nuts and cream!

2 tbsp butter	I tsp honey
I cup Amaretti cookies, crushed	3 tbsp cornstarch
I tbsp cocoa	150 ml (5 fl oz) milk
150 ml (5 fl oz) chocolate yoghurt	
2 tbsp chopped, roasted hazelnuts	
150 ml (5 fl oz)mascarpone cheese	
150 ml (5 fl oz) whipped cream	

1. Put the butter and the honey in a saucepan and melt slowly over a low heat.
2. Remove from the heat, add the crushed cookies and mix well.
3. Press the mixture into the bottom of a 7 inch removable-base flan tin, then set aside to cool.
4. Mix the cornstarch and cocoa together in a bowl using a little cold milk, then heat the remainder of the milk and pour it into the bowl gradually, stirring constantly.
5. Pour the mixture back into the saucepan and simmer until thickened, remove from the heat, stir in the yoghurt and hazelnuts, then pour the mixture onto the biscuit base.
6. Make the topping by mixing the cheese with the whipped cream, and whisking gently until thick.
7. Using a palette knife, spread the topping evenly over the Torte. Place in a refrigerator and chill until set.

Sprinkle with chocolate or cocoa powder and serve.

Autumn 2

FOREPLAY

Sweet & Savoury Potato Skins

THE MAIN EVENT

Tomato & Fennel Pork Chops in
Red Wine
Pumpkin Rice in Savoy Leaves

AFTERGLOW

Rum Syrup Oranges & Fresh Cream

Sweet & Savoury Potato Skins

It's amazing what you can do with a few skins.

2 large potatoes, scrub-washed	**cooking oil**
I large sweet potato, scrub-washed	**ground chilli pepper**

1. Peel the potatoes thickly and leave the skins to dry.
2. Heat in a large pan until very hot enough oil to deep fry the potato skins, then deep fry the skins until they are golden brown.
3. Remove the skins from the oil, drain off the excess oil onto kitchen paper and sprinkle them with chilli pepper.

Serve with a dip of your choice.

Tomato & Fennel Pork Chops in Red Wine

Juicy, succulent pork, cooked in a saucy blend of wine, tomatoes and fennel seeds.

2 large, lean pork chops	**½ onion, chopped**
½ tbsp fennel seeds	**125g (4 oz) tinned tomatoes**
90 ml (3 fl oz) vegetable stock	**90 ml (3 fl oz) red wine**
I tbsp lemon juice	**I tbsp olive oil**

1. Heat the oil in a frying pan and brown the pork chops on both sides then set aside.
2. Pour off excess oil, put the onions into the frying pan and sauté for 5 minutes.
3. Add the sugar, fennel seeds and tomatoes, then stir well.
4. Add the stock and bring to the boil.
5. Add the wine, lemon juice, salt and pepper to taste, then pour the sauce over the pork chops, cover and cook for 30 minutes in a preheated oven 350 F / 180 C / Gas Mark 4. Thicken the sauce with a little flour if preferred, cook for a further 5 minutes and serve.

Pumpkin Rice in Savoy Leaves

A dish to eat at the witching hour!

250g (8 oz) white rice
155g (5 oz) pumpkin, peeled, seeded and diced
1 savoy cabbage
600 ml (20 fl oz) water
½ skellion or spring onion thinly sliced
3 sprigs fresh thyme
knob of butter
salt and black pepper

1. Place a knob of butter in a pan, add the thinly cut skellion and fry gently on a low heat for a few seconds.
2. Dice the pumpkin into small cubes and add them to the pan.
3. Pour the water into the pan, add the thyme, two pinches of salt and black pepper then simmer on a medium heat for 10-15 minutes until the pumpkin begins to soften. Do not allow the pumpkin pieces to overcook.
4. Wash the rice thoroughly and it add to the pan.
5. Turn down the heat and leave to steam on low until the rice is fluffy and light and the pumpkin is cooked but firm. Add small amounts of boiling water at intervals if necessary.
6. Remove the heart from the cabbage and steam the outer leaves gently until cooked but still firm.

To serve, place the cabbage leaves upside down in a serving bowl and spoon on the rice.

Rum Syrup Oranges

Hot and zesty rum-soaked fruit. Delicious!

2 oranges
2 tbsp dark rum
30g (1oz) sugar
30ml (1 fl oz) water

1. Wash the oranges and dry them with a clean towel, then grate some rind from the oranges and arrange it evenly on an oven-proof dish.
2. Peel the oranges and slice them thickly and arrange the slices evenly over the dish on top of the rind.
3. Boil the sugar and water together until they form a thick syrup, remove the syrup from the heat, add the rum and mix together well.
4. Pour the syrup over the oranges and rind and place the dish in a pre-heated oven 350F / 180C / Gas Mark 4 for 10-15 minutes.

Serve hot with fresh single cream.

Coming Home To You (Soup)

A cold, black night descends at the end of a cold, grey day. Raising my collar against the chill wind, I plunge my hands deep inside my overcoat pockets in search of warmth. The road home seems endless to my tired feet, weary from the day's hard grind. As I wrestle to stay upright on a sidewalk cunningly littered with treacherous patches of ice, I have only one thing on my mind... you. The thought of coming home to you comforts and sustains me. As my feet switch to automatic pilot my mind begins to wander and, in my imagination, I am holding you. I can feel the tingling sensation in my fingertips that creeps through my hands and up my arms, as your heat defrosts my frozen limbs, slowly bringing my body back to life. Raising you to my lips I drink deeply, swallow, and feel your life-giving fluid seep through me, warming me from head to toe. My need for you grows, threatening to consume me. I drink again, and again, gulping you down urgently... until, finally, you are spent... and I am sated.

Oooh!! What wouldn't I give for a delicious cup of hot soup.

Winter I

FOREPLAY

Winter Vegetable Soup

THE MAIN EVENT

Winter Warmer
Creamy Herb Potatoes
Glazed Vegetables

AFTERGLOW

'Enticement' & Chocolate Sauce

(See photograph on pages 126-127)

Winter Vegetable Soup

A thick winter vegetable soup to warm the cockles of your heart!

I onion, chopped
I small carrot, peeled and diced
15g (½ oz) butter
220 ml (7 fl oz) vegetable stock
½ small turnip, peeled and diced
½ leek, scrub-washed and thinly sliced
I tsp tomato paste
salt and black pepper
fresh chopped parsley

1. Melt the butter in a saucepan, add the onions and sauté until soft, then add the carrots, turnips, stock and salt and pepper to taste.
2. Bring to the boil and simmer for 10 minutes then add the leeks and tomato paste, stir, cover and simmer for a further 15 minutes. Garnish with chopped parsley and serve.

Winter Warmer

A hearty meal to tantalise the tastebuds, nourish and sustain.

250g (8 oz) oxtail, chopped into bite-sized chunks
185g (6 oz) butter beans, fresh or canned
I spring onion
I clove garlic, crushed
3 sprigs fresh thyme
2 level tbsp all-purpose seasoning
I level tbsp curry powder
I tbsp olive oil
pinch of coarse ground black pepper
4 pimento seeds, crushed

1. Wash the oxtail thoroughly and place it in a pan.
2. Add the chopped spring onion, garlic, thyme, all-purpose seasoning, curry powder, black pepper, pimento seeds and cooking oil.

3. Mix everything together with a wooden spoon, then add a cupful of water.

4. Cover and leave to steam cook slowly for 1½ hours on a low heat, making sure that the liquid does not over-reduce by adding small amounts of boiling water if necessary.

5. If using dried butter beans, soak them over-night, boil them briskly for 10 minutes, then simmer them gently for 20-30 minutes. The butter beans may then be added to the pot of Winter Warmer after it has simmered for 15 minutes. If using canned butter beans, they should be added for the last 10 minutes of cooking time.

Creamy Herb Potatoes

Creamed potatoes flavoured with dill.

750g (1½ lb) potatoes, peeled, washed, cut into pieces
30g (1 oz) butter
60 ml (2 fl oz) hot milk
1 tbsp fresh, chopped dill
salt and black pepper

1. Place the potato pieces in a saucepan of cold, salted water then bring to the boil. Cook for 15 minutes until tender, then drain and transfer to a bowl.

2. Mash the potatoes with a fork or masher, sprinkle the dill on top, add the butter, hot milk, salt and pepper to taste then beat until smooth, creamy and fluffy. Reheat slowly, garnish with parsley and serve hot in scoops.

Glazed Vegetables

Sweet and succulent.

220g (7 oz) baby carrots
220g (7 oz) asparagus tips
60 g (2 oz) butter

1 tbsp brown sugar
½ tsp salt
fresh chopped parsley
salt and pepper

1. Put the carrots into enough water to cover and boil for 3 minutes.
2. Add the asparagus and boil for another 5 minutes until tender but firm.
3. Melt the butter in a pan, add the sugar, salt and pepper
4. Drain the vegetables and add them to the glaze mixture, stir and serve garnished with chopped parsley.

'Enticement'

A wicked dessert for certified chocoholics!

275g (10 oz) plain flour
2 tsp bicarbonate of soda
75g (3 oz) butter
250g (9 oz) soft light brown sugar
4 large eggs
100g (4 oz) unsweetened chocolate
200 ml (7 fl oz) milk
5 ml (1 tsp) vanilla essence
1 tbsp jam
250 ml (8 fl oz) whipping cream
pinch of salt
1 teaspoon chocolate or cocoa powder

1. Grease and line two 20 cm / 8 inch sandwich tins.
2. Sift the flour, soda and salt .
3. Cream the butter and sugar together until fluffy then gradually beat in the eggs.
4. Add the melted chocolate and beat well.
5. Fold in the flour, milk and vanilla at intervals and mix until smooth.
6. Divide the mixture evenly between the tins and level off.
7. Bake in a preheated oven at 180 C / 350 F / Gas Mark 4 for 30-40 minutes.

8. Turn out onto a cooling tray and allow to cool.
9. Spread a thin layer of jam on one cake, add a thick layer of whipped cream and sandwich together.
10. Whip up some more cream and pipe over the top of the cake, then sprinkle with powdered chocolate.

Keep chilled until ready to serve.

Chocolate Sauce

Chocolate sauce, with its finger-licking qualities, will always honour any dessert.

125g (4 oz) plain chocolate
30 ml (1 fl oz) milk
5 ml (1 tsp) vanilla essence
1 knob butter

1. Break up the chocolate and put it into a bowl, add the butter, then place the bowl over a saucepan of boiling water.
2. Stir the chocolate until it melts, then add the milk and vanilla essence.
3. Stir well and serve immediately.

If it feels good... do it!

Chocolate is the favourite sweet indulgence of millions of people all over the world.

A timeless association with all things romantic has made chocolates a popular gift on special occasions, like birthdays and anniversaries; especially where there is an emotional bond between the giver and the receiver.

Through countless generations the link between chocolate and love (especially erotic love) has endured. But why do we associate chocolate with eroticism?

One theory is that eating chocolate actually makes us feel romantic, because of a chemical called phenylethylamine. Present in chocolate in minute quantities, phenylethylamine is said to cause a chemical reaction in the body that produces the same effect in the brain as that of being in love.

This may or may not explain why chocolate is such a turn on, but, when it tastes and feels so good, who cares?

Winter 2

FOREPLAY

Stuffed Paratha
Saag (Spinach)

THE MAIN EVENT

Mutton Curry
Steamy Rice
Raita (Cucumber & Yoghurt)

AFTERGLOW

Shrikand

Stuffed Paratha

An Asian bread commonly eaten with curry.

225g (8 oz) wheat flour
220 ml (7 fl oz) water
45g (1½ oz) cooked peas

½ tsp salt
100g (4 oz) ghee

1. Sift the flour and salt into a mixing bowl then stir, gradually adding the water until a stiff dough is formed.
2. Flour a clean surface and knead the dough until it is smooth, then form into round balls.
3. Using a rolling pin, roll the dough balls into flat, thin circles, then spread the peas evenly over the surface, pressing them into the dough. Fold the dough over and roll it back into round balls, then cover the balls with a clean towel and allow them to stand for 30 minutes.
4. Lightly flour a clean surface and roll the balls of stuffed dough into ¼ inch thick circles.
5. Grease a frying pan lightly with melted ghee and fry each paratha over a medium heat, on both sides until golden brown. Keep warm in a preheated oven on low and serve hot as an accompaniment.

Saag (Spinach)

Spinach seasoned with Garam Masala. A delightful accompaniment to vegetarian or meat dishes..

220g (7 oz) frozen whole leaf spinach,
(or 440g (14 oz) fresh spinach, chopped)
30g (1 oz) ghee
½ tsp garam masala

1 onion, sliced
½ tsp salt

1. Melt the ghee in a saucepan, add the onions and fry gently until they are soft, then add the garam masala and salt to taste. Fry for 2-3 minutes, stirring constantly.
2. Add the frozen spinach, stir and cook until the spinach is completely defrosted (approximately 5 minutes). Stir well and serve hot.

Mutton Curry

A mutton dish that doesn't need to be dressed as lamb. It's beautiful as it is!

250g (8 oz) boneless mutton	**I tbsp white wine vinegar**
½ tsp ground chilli pepper	**½ tsp mustard seeds**
½ tsp ground ginger	**½ tsp ground cumin**
½ tsp ground coriander	**½ tsp tumeric**
25 ml (I oz) ghee	**I clove garlic, diced**
I small onion, chopped	**I small chilli, seeded and chopped**
I tsp salt	

1. Put the chilli powder, mustard seeds, ginger, tumeric, cumin and coriander into a mortar and pound, otherwise, place the ingredients into a mixing bowl and press with a spoon.
2. Add the vinegar and mix into a paste.
3. Heat the ghee in a saucepan, add the garlic, onion and chopped chilli and fry until brown.
4. Stir in the paste and cook for 3 minutes, stirring constantly.
5. Add the meat, sprinkle with the salt, stir well and cover.
6. Cook on a low heat for 2 hours until the mutton is tender, adding small amounts of boiled water if necessary.

Serve hot with accompaniments.

Steamy Rice

Some people find it difficult to cook white rice, this is how to do it!

250g (8 oz) white rice	**I tsp butter**
salt	**500 ml (16 fl oz) cold water**

1. Pour the rice into a sieve and wash thoroughly under the cold water tap then put the clean rice into a saucepan.
2. Pour the cold water over the rice covering I inch above the rice, then add the butter and salt to taste.
3. Stir, cover, put over a low heat and allow to cook slowly until light and fluffy, adding a little boiling water if the liquid dries out before the rice is cooked. Garnish with fresh herbs of your choice and serve hot.

Raita

Cool cucumber in creamy natural yoghurt!

(See the recipe on page 56.)

Shrikand

If you've got a sweet tooth this creamy Asian dessert should tickle your fancy!

150 ml (8 fl oz) natural yoghurt	2 tbsp sultanas
1 small can (150 ml / 5 fl oz) sweetened condensed milk	
¼ tsp ground cinnamon	¼ tsp ground nutmeg
3 tbsp chopped pistachio nuts	mint leaves for garnishing

1. Put the sultanas in water to soak for 15 minutes then strain them through a sieve and set them aside.
2. Mix the yoghurt and condensed milk together in a bowl, adding more of either ingredient according to taste, then add half the sultanas.
3. Spoon the mixture into a pyrex dish, place it over a pan of boiling water and steam it, uncovered, for 15-20 minutes until set. Test by touching the middle for firmness.
4. Remove the Shrikand from the heat, sprinkle the remainder of the sultanas on top then, sprinkle with the nutmeg, cinnamon and chopped pistachios.

Refrigerate and serve garnished with fresh mint leaves. Cut into wedges for individual portions.

Part 5

The shopping having been safely stowed in the back of the car, she opened the door on the passenger side and got in. Looking up, she was met by a pair of laughing eyes, filled with warmth. He leaned over and kissed her lightly on the mouth. Then, without saying a word, he started the engine, maneouvred the car out of its parking space and steered it out of the car park.

As he negotiated the traffic on the road home, she stole a glance at his reflection in the rear-view mirror. Struck, again, by the beauty of his face, she sighed contentedly, secure in the knowledge that marriage had not ended their love affair. The private games they played merely fuelled the fire that kept their passion for each other alive.

Tonight they would sleep in each other's arms, as they had for the past nine years – as she hoped they would for the rest of their lives.

THE END

You animal!

In Chinese astrology human beings are divided into 12 broad personality types, each with its own zodiac sign. Named after different animals, the 12 signs of the Chinese zodiac are: Rat, Ox, Tiger, Cat, Dragon, Snake, Horse, Goat, Monkey, Rooster, Dog and Pig.

Each of these signs spans a period of a complete Chinese calendar year (unlike Western astrology, which divides one year into 12 'star' signs), and the year in which you were born determines what kind of animal you are.

The Chinese year beginning 6 Feb 1970 and ending 26 Jan 1971 is the Year of the Dog; so people born between these dates are dogs! Anyone born between 28 Jan 1960 and 14 Feb 1961 (the Year of the Rat) is, therefore, a rat!

Since each sign has its own particular tastes and fancies, it might be worthwhile finding out what kind of animal you'll be entertaining.
Then, if you crave the thrill of the hunt, you can choose an appropriate menu, to bring out the beast in your date!

Pig & Rat

Are you dating a Rat? Is the love of your life a Pig?
If the answer to either of these questions is 'yes' this menu may be just what you're looking for. Both these signs have a taste for food that would be called 'delicacies', and they are both rather partial to a nice bordeaux. So, if you're planning on doing a spot of rat-catching, lay the right bait and make the rat come to you!

FOREPLAY

Mannish Water

THE MAIN EVENT

Roast Venison in Claret
Sauté Potatoes
Grape, Walnut &
Coriander Salad

AFTERGLOW

Sherry Pears à la Creme

(See photograph on pages 124-125)

Mannish Water

This rich soup is a Caribbean speciality. The entrails (traditionally the testicles), head and feet of the goat are boiled to a stock, seasoned and cooked down with vegetables. The soup is said to be vital for male virility!

800 ml (30 fl oz) water
250g (8 oz) goat's testicles, head and feet (mixed), cleaned and chopped
1 medium turnip, peeled, halved and sliced
1 cho-cho (christophine) seeded, peeled and sliced
1 carrot, peeled and sliced
½ hot fresh pepper
¼ tsp pimento seeds, crushed
1 skellion or spring onion, chopped
3 sprigs fresh thyme
salt to taste

1. Wash the meat, place it in a large saucepan with the water and boil to a stock for about 1 hour, strain and discard any bones add the skellion, thyme, crushed pimentos and salt to taste.
2. Add the turnip, cho-cho and carrots to the stock then bring to the boil.
3. Reduce the heat, add the fresh hot pepper to the pot.
4. Cover the pot and leave it to simmer until the vegetables are tender. Remove the hot pepper from the pot after 5 minutes cooking time.

Dumplings, yams and other vegetables can also be added to this soup if liked. Serve hot.

Roast Venison in Claret

Never eaten venison? You don't know what you're missing!

750g (1½ lb) loin of venison
30 ml (1 fl oz) claret
4 sprigs fresh thyme, chopped
1 tbsp plain flour

1 tbsp olive oil
1 onion, chopped
1 bay leaf
salt and coarse black pepper

1. Put the venison in a bowl, add the thyme (saving a little for garnishing), bayleaf and onions, then pour the claret over the loin of venison. Cover and leave to marinate overnight in the refrigerator.

2. Remove the venison from the marinade and place in a roasting tin, brush with the oil and cover completely with foil. Roast in a pre-heated oven 180 C / 350 F / Gas Mark 4 for approximately 1 hour, basting occasionally until cooked but still moist.

3. Meanwhile, pour the marinade into a saucepan, bring it to the boil and let it boil until the quantity reduces by half.

4. Strain the liquid, return it to a clean pan, add some of the roast juices to the pan, stir in the plain flour and cook until thickened. Remove the pan from the heat and add salt and pepper to taste.

5. Place the cooked venison on a serving plate and pour the rich gravy over and around the meat. Garnish with a little fresh thyme and serve with redcurrant jelly.

Sauté Potatoes

Perfect anytime.

500g (1 lb) potatoes, peeled, washed	**45g (1½ oz) butter**
1 tbsp vegetable oil	**salt and black pepper**

1. Put the peeled potatoes into salted, boiling water and allow to boil for 10 minutes.

2. Drain off the water and cut the potatoes into slices using a sharp knife.

3. Heat the butter and oil together in a frying pan and sauté the potatoes until golden brown.

4. Remove the potatoes from the pan, drain them on kitchen paper, then transfer the cooked potatoes to a warmed serving plate, sprinkle with salt and pepper, garnish with parsley and serve.

If you need to keep the potatoes warm until you are ready to serve them, put them in a preheated oven on low for a short period of time, then sprinkle them with parsley just before serving.

Coriander, Grape & Walnut Salad

An unusual combination of flavours to tantalise the tastebuds.

125g (4 oz) walnuts, halved
30g (1 oz) butter
½ crisp lettuce, separated and washed
75g (2½ oz) seedless grapes, black and green mix
225g (8 oz) cottage cheese
4 tbsp virgin olive oil
2 tbsp lemon juice
½ tsp ground coriander
salt and pepper

1. Melt the butter in a saucepan, add the walnuts and cook for 3 minutes, then remove the walnuts and set them aside.
2. Arrange the lettuce leaves in a serving bowl, then arrange the grapes, cottage cheese and cooked walnuts on top.
3. Put the olive oil into a bowl, add the coriander, lemon juice, salt and pepper to taste, beat the ingredients together and pour the dressing over the salad. Chill and serve.

Sherry Pears à la Creme

Make that for two!

2 firm, ripe pears, peeled, cored and thickly sliced
90 ml (3 fl oz) sherry
90 ml (3 fl oz) water
45g (1½ oz) caster sugar
½ lemon, rind and juice
½ cinnamon stick
1 clove
whipping cream
1 tbsp crushed almonds

1. Put the sherry, water, sugar, juice and rind of the lemon into a saucepan, add the cinnamon stick and cloves, stir until the sugar is melted then bring to the boil.
2. Add the slices of pear to the syrup and simmer for 3 minutes. Meanwhile, whip the cream.
3. Transfer the pears to a serving dish, boil the syrup until reduced to half the quantity, remove the cinnamon stick then pour the syrup over the pear slices.
4. Sprinkle the pears with the crushed almonds and serve with the whipped cream.

TITBIT...

Keep it up!

Vitamin C is not produced naturally in the body, so it has to be obtained from what we eat. Our main supplier of this important vitamin is fruit.

However, eating fruit doesn't only give your body a lift. According to popular myths and legends, eating fruit can also add zest to a flagging sex drive!

Throughout the ages, fruits of all kinds have been charged with causing sexual arousal. These include peaches, fresh figs, cherries, grapes and, of course, the humble apple (the oldest aphrodisiac of them all).

So, if you want to maintain a vigorous love life, remember: a fruit salad a day can keep flagging at bay!

Erotica!

The power to arouse sexual desire in humans has, at times, been attributed to various body parts of other living creatures.

With this in mind, here is a recipe containing some of the more exotic ingredients believed to enhance sexual performance.

Stir-fry Erotica

1 dried frog
1 tail of a young crocodile
2 sea slugs
2 goose tongues
2 testicles (any kind will do!)
2 tablespoons deer sperm
1 teaspoon extract of camel's hump
1 clove garlic (crushed)
1 large onion (chopped)
3 tablespoons virgin olive oil
sprig of parsley
salt and pepper to taste

1. Cut the dried frog, crocodile tail, sea slugs, goose tongues and testicles into bite-sized pieces (put to one side).
2. Heat virgin olive oil in a large frying pan until smoking.
3. Fry onions and garlic until soft, stirring continuously.
4. Add diced meats and continue stirring until tender.
5. Reduce heat and pour in deer sperm and stir for a further 2 minutes.
6. Turn out into a warmed serving dish. Sprinkle the top with extract of camel's hump. Garnish with parsley.

Serve with a selection of erotic vegetables and brace yourself for the impact!

Horse & Goat

Looking forward to a bit of after dinner horseplay? Then serve a meal that's fit for a horse! Horses and Goats are the vegetable-lovers of the zodiac, so this is a suitable menu for either of these signs. Goats have a reputation for liking foods that are bland, but this delicious meal should satisfy anyone who has a weakness for fresh vegetables. By the way... you might like to dress the dinner table with a spray or two of narcissus. It's their favourite flower.

FOREPLAY

Crispy Raw Vegetables
with Sweet & Sour Sauce

THE MAIN EVENT

Hot Vegetable Curry
Steamy Rice

AFTERGLOW

Minty Ice Cream

Crispy Raw Vegetables with Sweet & Sour Sauce

Healthy food doesn't have to be bland. Jazz it up with a titillating sauce. (Feel free to select alternative vegetables to suit your taste.)

2 carrots, peeled, washed and cut into thick strips
8-12 baby sweetcorn, washed
2 spring onions, trimmed and washed
½ crispy lettuce, washed
2 celery stalks, trimmed, washed and cut into thick strips

Cut the spring onions into strips then neatly arrange all the ingredients on a serving plate and serve with a small bowl of sweet and sour sauce for dipping.

For the Sweet & Sour Sauce:

An oriental sauce which can be served with a variety of dishes .

2 tbsp wine vinegar	**2 tbsp clear honey**
1 tbsp tomato paste	**2 tbsp sherry**
1 tsp sweet chilli sauce	**2 tbsp cornflour**

1. Put all the ingredients into a bowl, mix them together, then transfer the mixture to a small saucepan and cook gently for 5 minutes, stirring constantly.
2. Transfer the mixture into a small round serving dish and serve.

Hot Vegetable Curry

A authentic, spicy vegetable inferno, from Burma.

2 medium potatoes, peeled, washed and cubed
2 carrots, peeled, washed and diced
½ aubergine, washed and cut into ½ inch slices
200 ml (6½ fl oz) water   **4 cauliflower florets**
2 tbsp vegetable oil   **chopped fresh coriander**

½ onion, sliced   I garlic clove, crushed
¼ inch fresh ginger, peeled and diced
½ tsp chilli powder   ¼ tsp turmeric
2 tomatoes, chopped   ½ fresh chilli, diced
2 tbsp natural yoghurt   salt

1. Wash all the vegetables and set them aside.
2. Heat the oil, add the onions, garlic, chilli pepper and turmeric then stir fry for 5 minutes.
3. Add the water, tomatoes, coriander and potatoes, bring to the boil then reduce the heat and simmer until the potatoes are par-cooked.
4. Add the aubergine and carrot, simmer for another 3 minutes, then add the cauliflower.
5. Add salt to taste, simmer until all the vegetables are cooked then remove from the heat and serve topped with yoghurt.

Serve with rice. (See the recipe for Steamy Rice on page 103.)

Minty Ice-cream

Cool down after a hot meal with this iced treat.

300 ml (10 fl oz) milk   300 ml (10 fl oz) double cream
90g (3 oz) caster sugar   2 eggs, beaten
3 drops mint essence   fresh mint leaves to garnish

1. Put the beaten eggs into a mixing bowl, then heat the milk and sugar together in a saucepan and pour onto the eggs, stirring briskly until well mixed.
2. Return the saucepan to the heat and cook the mixture slowly, stirring constantly until thick and creamy. Cover and set aside to cool.
3. When cooled, drop the mint essence into the mixture and stir well, then whip the double cream and fold it into the mixture.
4. Pour the mixture into a container and freeze for 1 hour until it is set but not too firm.
5. Remove the ice-cream from the freezer and beat it until the ice crystals have gone.
6. Freeze for a further 2 hours until set firm. Scoop into ice cream bowls to serve and garnish with fresh mint leaves.

Heat (Curry)

You're really hot. You make me burn
My body's damp and clammy
Sweat's breaking out from every pore
And trickling down my cammy

And, though it brings another flush,
Each mouthful I do savour
I just can't seem to get enough
Of your distinctive flavour

Your size is somewhat daunting
Don't know if I can take it
I'll have to give it my best shot
But am I going to make it?

I'm trying to cram it all inside
There's no space left to fill!
Why don't I just cry "Stop! Enough!"?
I haven't got the will

I'm really under pressure
Is it ever going to end?
(Perhaps I'd have done better
To share you with a friend!)

At last! You're done!! It's over!!!
I'm laying down my fork
So stuffed and so uncomfortable
That I can barely walk

You'd think I'd learn from past mistakes
Yet, somehow, I persist
It really begs the question
Am I a masochist?

Snake & Cat

Aspiring snake-charmers should note that the sophisticated Snake absolutely adores caviar. Cats are also great lovers of all things fishy. Something else these two signs have in common is a preference for cool colours; like ice blue and grey. So, wearing an alluring outfit in these tones could add to your charms. (There's more than one way to skin a cat!)

FOREPLAY

Caviar & Crackers

THE MAIN EVENT

Tarragon Salmon with
Hollandaise Sauce
Potatoes au Gratin
Avocado & Beef Tomato Salad

AFTERGLOW

Flamed Cherries

Tarragon Salmon in White Wine

A quick and easy 'gourmet' dish for any occasion.

2 large salmon steaks
fresh tarragon, chopped
90 ml (3 fl oz) white wine
butter
salt and black pepper

1. Wash the fish steaks, place them in an oven dish, pour the wine over them, then sprinkle with the chopped tarragon, salt and black pepper to taste.
2. Using a palette knife, put little knobs of butter on each fish steak.
3. Pre-heat the grill and grill the fish steaks under a medium heat for 10-15 minutes on each side until cooked through but still tender and moist. At intervals, baste the fish with the juices.
Serve hot with Hollandaise sauce.

Hollandaise Sauce

A tribute to any seafood combination, quick and easy to make!

3 egg yolks
2 tbsp white wine vinegar
100g (3½ oz) butter
¼ tsp salt
black pepper

1. Put the egg yolks and wine vinegar into a bowl.
2. Place the bowl over a saucepan of hot water and mix the ingredients together, heating gently until they thicken.
3. Add half the butter and whisk the mixture until the butter is melted.
4. Add the remainder of the butter and whisk until thick.

5. Remove the sauce from the heat, add salt and pepper to taste and serve hot.

Potatoes au Gratin

A popular dish served as an accompaniment to many a meal but still considered highly desirable.

2-3 medium potatoes, peeled and sliced
60g (2 oz) Cheddar cheese, grated
30g (1 oz) white bread crumbs
salt
ground paprika
fresh chopped parsley

1. Sprinkle the sliced potatoes evenly with salt and arrange them in layers in a greased oven dish.
2. Melt the butter in a saucepan and pour it over the potatoes, then sprinkle the grated cheese and the breadcrumbs evenly over the top.
3. Bake in a pre-heated oven 200 C / 400 F / Gas Mark 6 for 45 minutes until cooked through and golden on top. Garnish with parsley or a herb of your choice and serve hot.

Avocado & Beef Tomato Salad

1 large avocado, peeled, stoned and sliced
1 large beef tomato, washed, halved and then sliced thinly
1 spring onion, cut into thin strips

1. Neatly arrange the avocado and tomato slices onto a serving dish, sprinkle the strips of spring onion over the top evenly.
2. Pour on the dressing of your choice and serve.

Flamed Cherries

Oooooh... light my fire

1 punnet sweet, ripe cherries
3 tbsp brown sugar
juice of 1 lime
90 ml (3 fl oz) brandy

1. Wash the cherries, place them in a pyrex bowl, baste them in the lime juice and half of the brandy, then sprinkle the sugar on top, stir and leave them to sit a warm place for 2 hours.
2. After 2 hours, place the bowl over boiling water and gently heat the cherries in the bowl until they are warm.
3. When ready to serve, pour the remainder of the brandy over the cherries and set them alight.

Serve with rich vanilla ice cream.

Cream

Milky
Frothy
Swirling
Foaming
Free and single
Folded double
Thick and clotted
Stiff from whipping
Aaahh......................cream!

Photographs of the menus below are shown in the following pages:

AUTUMN I (from page 79)
Steamy Bream, Boiled Dumplings & Yams, Callaloo

PIG & RAT (from page 107)
Mannish Water, Roast Venison in Claret, Coriander, Grape & Walnut
Salad, Sherry Pears à la Creme

WINTER I (from page 95)
'Winter Warmer', Creamy Herb Potatoes, Glazed Vegetables

WINTER DESSERT
'Enticement' with Chocolate Sauce

Dog & Rooster

Calling all dog-lovers! Meat is the way to this particular animal's heart. Dogs and Roosters just love to eat meat. Feed these carniverous beasts a meal of succulent prime cuts, and have them eating out of your hand!

FOREPLAY

Spicy Pork Balls
with Peanut Sauce

THE MAIN EVENT

Steak & Oyster Pie
Courgette Fritters

AFTERGLOW

Rum Cheesecake

Spicy Pork Balls

220g (7oz) minced pork
I small onion, finely diced
I small garlic clove, diced
¼ hot fresh pepper, seeded and diced
I tsp dried thyme
I egg, beaten
I tbsp plain flour
cooking oil
salt and black pepper

1. Place the minced pork in a bowl then add the garlic, hot pepper, thyme, salt and pepper and mix together well.
2. Next, stir the beaten egg into the mixture.
3. Put a generous amount of oil into a frying pan heat it until very hot.
4. On a floured surface, roll the meat mixture into balls using the palms of your hands.
5. Drop the pork balls into the oil and fry them turning constantly until they are cooked and golden brown. If necessary fry them in two batches.
6. To keep the cooked pork balls warm until ready or serve or whilst you cook a second batch, put them in a serving dish and keep them warm in a preheated oven at moderate heat.

Serve with peanut sauce.

Peanut Sauce

6 tbsp water
2 tbsp crunchy peanut butter
I tbsp soy sauce
I tbsp lemon
dash chilli sauce

1. Add the water to the peanut butter, beating in 1 tablespoon at a time until smooth.

2. Add the soy sauce, lemon juice and chilli sauce to taste, then transfer to a small serving bowl to serve.

Steak and Oyster Pie

A meat-lover's dream come true!

> **500g (1 lb) ready made puff pastry**
> **450g (14 oz) beef, trimmed and cubed**
> **285 ml (9 fl oz) vegetable stock**
> **200 ml (6½ fl oz) stout**
> **1 small onion, chopped**
> **55g (2 oz) mushrooms, cleaned and sliced**
> **3 oysters**
> **2 tbsp olive oil**
> **1½ tbsp plain flour**
> **1 egg, beaten**
> **salt and freshly ground black pepper**

1. To make the pie filling: heat 1 tablespoon of the oil in a saucepan and fry the onions until soft, then remove the onions and set them aside.
2. Put the remainder of the oil into the pan and fry the steak pieces, then remove the steak and onions from the pan and set them aside.
3. Next, stir the flour into the pan, then gradually add the stock and Guinness, stirring continuously. Bring to the boil, then return the chopped onions and meat to the pan.
4. Add seasoning to taste, reduce the heat, cover and cook on a low heat until the meat is tender.
5. When the meat is cooked, add the mushrooms, cook for a further 5-10 minutes, then remove from the heat, set aside and allow to cool for 1 hour.
6. Open the oysters and add them to the meat together with their juices, add salt and pepper to taste and transfer the steak and oyster mixture to a pie dish, pour on some of the liquid, then brush the edge of the pie dish with water in preparation for the pastry cover.
7. On a clean, floured surface, roll the ready-made puff pastry into a large rectangle and cover the pie dish surface completely then, trim the

excess pastry away from the edges and press firmly around the dish edges to seal the pastry to the dish.

8. Use the excess pastry to make a pattern on the top of the pie, brush the surface with beaten egg to glaze and put the pie into a pre-heated oven, 220 C / 425 F / Gas Mark 7 and bake until the pastry is golden brown (30-45 minutes).

Courgette Fritters

2 courgettes, washed, trimmed and thickly sliced
75g (2½ oz) plain flour
I egg
vegetable oil for frying
cold water
salt and black pepper

1. To make the batter: sieve the flour and the salt into a bowl, then make a well in the centre of the flour and gradually mix in a few tablespoons of water and I tablespoon of oil, add the egg and whisk until the mixture becomes smooth.

2. Put the courgette slices into a bowl of boiling water and allow them to stand for I minute only, then remove them from the bowl, drain them and set them aside.

3. Put a generous amount of oil in a saucepan and allow it to heat well. When the oil is hot, dip the courgette slices into the batter, then deep fry until cooked through and crispy on the outside.

4. Place the fried courgettes onto clean kitchen roll to drain-off the excess oil, sprinkle with salt and black pepper, then serve hot and crispy.

Rum Cheesecake

Sultanas, rum and soft cheese create this exotic cheesecake.

60 ml (2 fl oz) white rum,
45g (1½ oz) sultanas, washed

65g (2 oz) melted butter or margarine
150g (5 oz) digestive biscuits, crushed
225g (8 oz) soft cheese
½ tsp vanilla flavouring
125g (4 oz) caster sugar
300 ml (10 fl oz) whipping cream or double cream

1. Put the sultanas and rum into a pan and boil for 3 minutes, then set aside to cool.

2. Mix together the melted butter and crushed digestives, spoon them into the base of an 8 inch flan dish and press them down to make the cheesecake base, then place in the fridge for approximately 30 minutes until firm.

3. Put the cheese in a bowl and beat it, gradually adding the caster sugar and vanilla.

4. Strain any excess liquid from sultanas, add them to the cheese mixture and stir.

5. Whip the cream and fold it into mixture evenly.

6. Remove the biscuit base from refrigerator, spoon the mixture on and level the surface.

7. Refrigerate for approximately 2 hours, then serve well chilled.

What am I?

Two of my first in rhubarb you'll find
My next is in orange (though not in the rind)
Missing from scallop, my third is in clam
My fourth letter's stuffed in the middle of ham
My fifth is in lentils, when not in a stew
My sixth is in carrots and celery, too
My last is in oysters and eels, but not trout
I am what Valentines Day's all about!

(Answer = R.O.M.A.N.C.E)

Oysters

Upon a bed of water you lay
Quivering
Clutching your precious pearls
Close to your heart
Pearls that will one day grace a maiden's neck
And nestle between her breasts

Upon a bed of water you lay
Waiting
Waiting to be taken
By men of the sea
Whose coming is as imminent
As it is guaranteed

Upon a bed of ice you will be laid
Enticing
Offered on a platter
To be ravaged hungrily
By those in search of inspiration...
For sexual gratification

Upon a bed of ice you will be laid
Knowing
In an instant it will be over
Their appetites whetted
They will devour you
Solely for their pleasure

Upon a bed of ashes you will lay
Discarded
A broken, empty shell devoid of riches
Sacrificed to the lust of man
The hollow left when all your juice is gone
Sucked dry of sustenance then thrown away

Monkey & Tiger

The ferocious Tiger is just a big pussycat with a very sweet tooth! Fruit pie is the favourite food of this noble beast, as it is for the mischievous Monkey. Indulge their passion for sweets with generous helpings of this dessert, and they'll be yours for the taking! The scent of jasmine in the air may be an aid to seduction when entertaining tigers and monkeys, as it is the favourite fragrance of both these signs.

FOREPLAY

Red Cherry Soup

THE MAIN EVENT

Guinea Fowl Fricassee
Cornbread

AFTERGLOW

Cinnamon Apple Pie

Red Cherry Soup

A maverick soup, for when you fancy something a little bit different.

220g (7 oz) cherries
600 ml (20 fl oz) water
1 tsp cornflour
15g (½ oz) sugar
1 tsp lemon juice
2 tbsp red wine
2 tbsp whipped cream

1. Put the cherries into a saucepan then, pour on the water and simmer for about 5-10 minutes until they are tender.
2. Sieve the cooked cherries, pushing them through with a wooden spoon to release the juices then, return the juice to the heat, bring it to boil and leave it to simmer gently.
3. Meanwhile, mix the cornflour and sugar together with a little water until smooth, then add it to the soup, stir and cook for 10 minutes.
4. Add the lemon juice and red wine to taste, then set aside to cool. Serve at room temperature, garnished with whipped cream.

Guinea Fowl Fricassee

Heavenly!!

1.5 kg (3 lb) whole guinea fowl, ready-to-cook
400 ml (13 fl oz) cold water
½ tsp whole allspice
1 onion, cut into four wedges
5 sprigs fresh thyme
1 bayleaf
2 chervils
2 carrots, peeled and sliced
2 spring onions, trimmed and chopped
2 tbsp flour
30g (1oz) butter
salt and pepper
fresh chopped parsley

1. Put the guinea fowl into a deep saucepan and add the water, allspice, onions, thyme, bayleaf, chervils, salt and pepper to taste. Bring to the boil, reduce the heat then cover and allow to simmer gently for about 20 minutes.
2. Remove the saucepan from the heat and set it aside to cool. When cooled, transfer the guinea fowl to a plate, then strain the stock and pour 200 ml (6½ fl oz) into a jug and set it aside.
3. Strip the skin from the guinea fowl and discard it, then trim the meat from the bones and cut it into neat pieces.
4. Put the butter in a saucepan, add the spring onions and carrots, then sauté them for a few minutes until the onions are soft. Remove the vegetables from saucepan using a slotted spoon and set them aside.
5. Stir the flour into the butter and cook for 2 minutes stirring continuously, then gradually stir in the stock. Bring to the boil stirring continuously until the sauce thickens.
6. Add the guinea fowl pieces to the sauce, then add the spring onions and carrots, cover and allow to simmer for 15-20 minutes.
7. Transfer to a warm serving dish, garnish with parsley and serve hot.

Cornbread

A delicious sweet bread to eat with savoury dishes.

125g (4 oz) plain flour
125g (4 oz) cornmeal
45g (1½ oz) caster sugar
1 tbsp baking powder
¼ tsp ground nutmeg
1 egg, lightly beaten
155 ml (5 fl oz) milk
75g (2½ oz) butter, melted then cooled

1. Put the flour, cornmeal, baking powder, sugar, nutmeg and salt into a mixing bowl and mix together well.
2. In a small bowl, add the melted butter to the beaten egg, mix in the milk and stir well, then pour the butter mixture into the flour and blend it together.
3. Grease a 20.5 cm (8 inch) cake tin, pour the mixture into the tin and spread evenly.

137

4. Place the tin in a pre-heated oven, 220 C / 425 F / Gas Mark 7 and bake for 25-30 minutes until cooked. Remove from the oven allow to cool, slice and serve.

Cinnamon Apple Pie

Just like mama used to make!

225g (8 oz) ready to use shortcrust pastry
750g (1½ lb) cooking apples, peeled, cored and sliced
155g (5 oz) sugar
½ tsp ground cinnamon
2 tsp lemon juice
30g (1 oz) plain flour
15g (½ oz) butter

1. Cut the pastry in half and on a clean, lightly floured surface, roll half of the pastry out and line a 23 cm (9 in) circular pie dish.
2. Arrange half the apple slices onto the pastry base. Put the sugar, flour, cinnamon and lemon juice into a bowl, mix them together, then spoon half the mixture over the apple slices. Repeat the process with another layer of apples and a final layer of cinnamon mixture. Then, using a palette knife, cover the pie filling with little knobs of the butter.
3. Roll the other half of the pastry out and using a shaped pastry cutter, cut out an attractive pattern. Damp the edges of the pie base and carefully place the patterned pastry over the top of the pie. Cut away any excess pastry from the edges and pinch press the edges together until sealed.
4. Arrange the pieces of cut pastry on top of the pie and brush with beaten egg or milk then bake in a pre-heated oven 220 C / 425 F / Gas Mark 7 for 40 minutes until cooked and golden brown.

Serve hot or cold with freshly whipped cream, ice-cream or custard.

Dragon & Ox

You don't need a big sword to slay a dragon. A juicy piece of beef will do very nicely! In common with the strapping Ox, the fiery Dragon shares a love of red meat. After a hearty meal of tender beef steak you won't be the one chasing the dragon... the dragon will probably be chasing you!

FOREPLAY

Tofu Consommé

THE MAIN EVENT

Steak Furieux
Sauté Potatoes

AFTERGLOW

SherryTrifle

Tofu Consommé

A delicious bean curd soup, for fans of tofu.

600 ml (20 fl oz) vegetable stock, cold
60g (2 oz) tofu (bean curd)
I spring onion, chopped
I egg white, beaten lightly
½ tbsp dry sherry
I bouquet garni
2 whole black peppercorns
I carrot
½ turnip, peeled and chopped

1. Peel the carrot, cut it in half and chop one half finely.
2. Put the stock, tofu, onion, carrot, turnip, peppercorns, bouquet garni and egg white into a saucepan and bring to the boil, stirring gently.
2. Reduce the heat to low and stir in the sherry, then simmer gently for 20 minutes.
3. Remove the saucepan from the heat and set it aside to cool. When cooled, skim off any scum on the surface, using a spoon, and strain the liquid through a clean muslin cloth or fine sieve.
4. Take the remaining half of the carrot and shred it into thin strips. Warm the consommé gently to serve hot, or serve cold, garnished with the strips of raw carrot.

Steak Furieux

Lean meat, marinated in ginger and garlic, grilled and topped with stir-fried vegetables.

2 sirloin steaks
I onion, sliced
½ green sweet pepper, seeded and sliced
8 green olives
4 large flat mushrooms, sliced
3 tbsp soy sauce

3 tbsp olive oil
¼ tsp ground ginger
¼ tsp ground garlic
2 tbsp black peppercorns, crushed
15g (½ oz) plain flour

1. Wash the steaks and soften them with a mallet, pat them dry with a clean tea towel and place in a bowl. Mix together the soy sauce, ground ginger and ground garlic, pour over the steak, cover and marinate for 20 minutes.

2. Sprinkle enough flour on a clean surface to flour the steaks. Remove the steaks from the marinade, drain them, flour both sides and press the black pepper, deeply and evenly into the steaks with the back of a spoon.

Meat
(Steak)

They say you're good for me
They say you're bad for me
What do they know?

Go mad if I have you?
Go mad if I don't!
What do I do?

The sight of you laid out before me
Excites my every sense
Hot
Sizzling
I take you in my mouth

Your blood red juices caress my tongue
And trickle from my lips

I savour your exquisite tenderness
And I am satisfied.

3. Pre-heat the grill, set it on a medium heat and grill the steaks on both sides until cooked to your liking.

4. While the steak are cooking, heat the oil in a pan and add the onions, mushrooms, olives and sweet pepper and stir-fry for 3 minutes then pour the marinade onto the vegetables, cover, lower the heat and simmer for 2 more minutes.

5. Remove the steaks from the grill, place them onto warm serving plates, then spoon the cooked vegetables over and serve hot with Sauté Potatoes and a side salad.

Sauté Potatoes

(See recipe on page 109.)

Sherry Trifle

Although this dessert is well-known and commonly served, it maintains a popular place in culinary circles; easy to make and delectably creamy to eat.

> **1 packet strawberry jelly**
> **4 fingers trifle cake slices**
> **100 ml (4 fl oz) sherry**
> **1 large can sliced peaches**
> **300 ml (11 fl oz) boiling water**
> **300 ml (11 fl oz) cold water**
> **250 ml (8 fl oz) whipping cream**
> **2 tbsp chopped almonds**

1. Put the trifle cake slices into a bowl, pour on the sherry and allow the cake to absorb the liquid.

2. Place the jelly into a measuring jug and pour on the boiling water then stir until dissolved.

3. Add the cold water to the liquid and stir. Transfer the jelly to a glass

bowl, then put the trifle cakes into the jelly and push them down gently until they are soaked in jelly.

3. Place the peach slices in the jelly in a pattern, then refrigerate and allow the trifle to set.

4. Remove the trifle from the fridge, whip the cream and cover the trifle with it. Sprinkle with chopped nuts and serve.

What am I?

My first is in sugar and also in sweet
My next's out of honey, but always in heat
My third in asparagus appears three times
My fourth you will find in the centre of limes
My fifth is in olives, but isn't in melons
My sixth is in nectarines, oranges and lemons
End with an 'A' and you will discover
An ingredient needed to be a great lover!

(Answer= S.T.A.M.I.N.A)

Quench it!

Drinks to steam you up or cool you down.

Irish Moss

Made from seaweed, this drink is said to put lead in one's pencil!

25g (1 oz) dried Irish moss	**1 litre (35 fl oz) water**
sugar to taste	**½ tsp rum**
125 ml (4 oz) milk	**¼ tsp grated nutmeg**
2 tbsp strawberry syrup (optional)	

1. Soak the Irish moss for a few hours in some water then simmer it on medium heat until tender.
2. Pour the remainder of the water in the pan and bring it to the boil.
3. Remove from the heat and strain through a clean muslin cloth or fine sieve.
4. Add sugar to taste, then add the rum, milk, nutmeg and syrup.
5. Transfer to a jug or bowl and refrigerate. Serve chilled.

'Quenched'

Non-alcoholically refreshing.

3 limes, thinly sliced	**75g (2½ oz) demerara sugar**
5 ml (¼ fl oz) boiling water	**500 ml (16 fl oz) cold bottled water**
1 drop vanilla essence	**ice**

1. Put the sliced limes into a jug and add the sugar and a drop of vanilla essence.
2. Pour on the boiling water, stir and allow to stand for 5 minutes.
3. Add the cold water, stir and refrigerate.
4. Serve with lots of ice.

Crucial Carrot Drink

Gets a 'kick' out of ginger!

75g (2½ oz) fresh ginger, peeled and crushed
4 carrots, juiced   **sugar to sweeten**
480 ml (16 fl oz) water

1. Boil the crushed ginger in 200 ml (7 fl oz)water for 5 minutes.
2. Transfer the liquid to a jug, allow it to cool, then mix it with the juice from the carrots.
3. Add 280 ml (9 fl oz) water, sweeten to taste, chill and serve.

'Lust'

Satisfies the craving!

250 ml (7 fl oz) white rum   **1 tsp sugar**
2 chopped bananas   **2 tbsp lime juice**

Blend with ice in a blender.

Nirvana

A wickedly tangy cocktail.

125 ml (4 oz) tequila   **1 tbsp Grenadine**
4 tbsp lemon juice

Shake well in a cocktail shaker and serve with ice.

'Lady in Red'

Sophisticated and elegant.

50 ml (1½ oz) white rum   125 ml (4 fl oz) tomato juice
lemon juice   tabasco sauce
worcester sauce

1. Shake all the ingredients together and strain into a wine glass.
2. Add salt and fresh, coarse ground black pepper to taste.

Sangria

Orange juice, sweet red wine and a burnt orange, create this popular Spanish drink.

1 litre (35 fl oz) orange juice   500 ml (17 fl oz) sweet red wine
1 large orange

1. Mix the orange juice and the wine together in a bowl.
2. Wash the outer skin of the orange to remove any dirt, then pierce it with a long fork and hold it over a medium flame, turning it until it is evenly burnt all over.
3. Add the hot orange to the bowl, cover with a clean, dry towel and leave to stand for 2-3 hours before serving well chilled.

Guinness Punch

It's vigorous, stout and packs a punch!

1 large can Guinness   1 can Nourishment or Nutriment
½ tsp vanilla essence   ½ tsp freshly grated nutmeg
1 small can (150 ml / 5 fl oz) condensed milk

1. Pour the Nourishment/Nutriment into a jug, add the vanilla essence, nutmeg and condensed milk, then stir well.
2. Gradually pour in the Guinness, stirring constantly to blend.

Refrigerate and serve with lots of ice.

The Morning After
(Alcohol)

I awake to the cold light of dawn
And I ask myself
Why did I do it?
I swore I'd never touch you again
After what you did to me last time
But time, and poor recollection, dull the pain
Of our last night of heady abandon
And, somehow, it's the nice things about you
That I recall, and am drawn to once more...
Your smell. Your taste.
The way you make me feel
When you're inside me
My inhibitions melt away
As you fill me with your fire
I feel a freedom unknown in more sober times
I know what it is to spread my wings and fly...until
The morning after
When my aching body tries to raise itself
From my dishevelled bed
Only to find that my legs, weak and trembling,
Struggle to support me
When the smell of you, lingering on my skin,
Makes my stomach churn
And every sound I hear
Assaults my throbbing head
'Tis then I swear the solemn oath of fools...
I will never, ever touch a drop of alcohol again!!!

You want more?

This selection of additional recipes can be used as alternatives or additions to those given as part of the set menu dishes.

Be adventurous, do your own thing!

SOUPS

Cod & Potato Soup

This clear soup with a mixture of textures and flavours makes a meal in itself.

> 1 skinless, boneless cod fillet
> 500 ml (16 fl oz) vegetable stock
> 1 large potato, peeled, washed and diced
> 1 carrot, peeled and chopped
> 1 stalk spring onion, thinly sliced
> 1 small turnip, peeled and washed
> 2 sprigs fresh thyme
> salt and black pepper

1. Wash and dice the cod then set it aside.
2. Put the stock into a saucepan and bring it to the boil.
3. Add the carrots, turnip, potatoes and fresh thyme, then cover and simmer for ten minutes.
4. When vegetables are nearly cooked, add the fish and simmer for another 15 minutes.
5. Add salt and pepper to taste.

Serve hot

Thai Noodle Soup

Tiger prawns swimming in noodles, herbs and spices.

10 tiger prawns, peeled
30g (1 oz) Thai noodles
6 whole cherry tomatoes, skinned
220 ml (7 oz) chicken stock
½ garlic clove, diced
½ inch root ginger, peeled and chopped
½ inch lemon grass, sliced thinly
1 spring onion, trimmed and sliced
½ tsp sugar
chilli sauce (to taste)
1 tsp lime juice
1 tsp coriander leaves, chopped
salt

1. Put the noodles in a saucepan of boiling, salted water and cook for 2 minutes then remove, drain and rinse through with hot water.
2. Pour the chicken stock into a saucepan, allow it to simmer then add the garlic, ginger and lemon grass. Let it simmer for another 5 minutes to bring out the flavour then strain it into another saucepan.
3. Bring the liquid back to the boil and add the prawns, spring onions, sugar and chilli sauce (to taste), then simmer for a further 5 minutes.
4. Add the tomatoes and lime juice and simmer for 3 minutes more.

Serve hot.

SAUCES

Rum & Cherry Sauce (Sweet)

A wonderful sauce for Christmas desserts, enjoyable all year round.

150g (5 oz) cherries, washed, stoned
30 ml (1 oz) dark rum
30g (1 oz) sugar
¾ tsp cornflour
½ tsp almond essence

1. Put the cherries, rum, sugar and cornflour into a saucepan and heat, stirring constantly, until the cherries soften and the mixture thickens.
2. Stir in the almond essence, remove from the heat and serve.

Yoghurt & Mustard Sauce (Savoury)

Cooling yoghurt, with a sting. For dipping.

225 ml (7 oz) yoghurt, natural
1 small onion, finely chopped
1 tbsp English mustard
1 tbsp chives, chopped

1. Put the yoghurt, onion, mustard, salt and pepper into a saucepan heat and stir gently for 10 minutes without boiling.
2. Remove from the heat, pour into a serving bowl and sprinkle with the chives.

ACCOMPANIMENTS

Chinese Fried Rice

This oriental classic integrates well with foods from all cultures.

150g (5 oz) long grain rice	125g (4 oz) peeled prawns
60g (2 oz) button mushrooms, sliced diagonally	
200g (7 oz) canned water chestnuts, drained, sliced	
2 spring onions	1 egg, beaten
2 tsp cold water	1 garlic clove, diced
1 tbsp oyster sauce	1 tsp fresh chopped parsley
salt and black pepper	2 tbsp cooking oil

1. Put approximately 375 ml (13 oz) of water into a saucepan and add ¼ tsp of salt then bring to the boil.
2. Wash the rice through a sieve, under cold water, add to the boiling

What am I?

My name and identity
Hide in this riddle
I'm hard on the outside
But soft in the middle
My brittle exterior
Cracks easily.
I'm really quite fragile
(Be gentle with me!)
Oozing and runny
When I'm opened up
Curvaceous in shape
I fit an E-cup

So versatile when
I come out of my shell
I get hard when I'm heated
When beaten I swell
I've often been used
As a sexual aid
I'm rich and I'm healthy
(I always get laid!)
A natural source
And supplier of 'E'
I'm yours for the taking
Go to work on me!!

(Answer = EGG)

water and simmer for 10-12 minutes. When cooked, spread the rice onto a large plate and allow to cool.

3. Put the beaten egg into a bowl with 2 teaspoons of water then put the cooking oil into a wok or pan and heat until it is very hot.

4. Add the egg and swirl until it resembles an omelette, remove the omelette from the heat and cut it into small squares.

5. Heat the remainder of the oil in the wok or pan until hot and add the onions, garlic and mushrooms then stir-fry for 2 minutes. Add the oyster sauce, water chestnuts and the prawns and continue to stir-fry for 1 more minute.

6. Add the cooled rice and stir-fry for 1 minute. Add the egg pieces and stir-fry for a further 1-2 minutes until all the ingredients are well mixed and hot.

Serve immediately with a meat, fish, vegetable stir-fry or the main dish of your choice.

Crucial Rice & Peas

Beans and rice steam-cooked in coconut and seasoning.

75g (2½ oz) black eye beans	**315g (11 oz) white rice**
55g (2 oz) creamed coconut	**1 spring onion**
3 sprigs fresh thyme	**salt and black pepper**
water	

1. Soak the black-eye beans overnight in water. Place the beans in fresh water, bring them to boil then simmer them for about 1 hour until they are cooked, adding boiled water if necessary (do not allow them to boil dry). Next add the chopped onions, black pepper, salt and creamed coconut to the beans and their liquid.

2. Wash the rice thoroughly in a small-holed sieve allowing the starch to wash out, then add it to the seasoned liquid.

3. Make sure the liquid covers the rice by approximately 2 inches, then reduce the heat, cover the pot and allow the rice to steam cook, testing the grains regularly and, if necessary, adding small amounts of boiled water at a time until the rice is fluffy and light.

Serve hot with meat, fish or vegetable main dishes.

MAIN DISHES

Lamb with Olives

Lamb steaks, fried and mixed with peppers and sensual olives, create this succulent, tender dish.

2 boneless lamb steaks, 2 cm (½ inch) thick
I green sweet pepper, seeded and chopped
125g (4 oz) stoned Greek olives
juice of I lemon
salt and coarse ground black pepper
2 tbsp olive oil

1. Wash the lamb steaks and season them with salt and black pepper
2. Pour the oil into a pan heat it until fairly hot
3. Fry the lamb steaks until they are brown on both sides, then set them aside, reduce the heat, add the peppers and olives and fry them until they are soft.
4. Stir in the lemon juice, return the lamb steaks to the pan, simmer gently for 10 minutes and serve hot.

Carib Chicken

A taste of the Caribbean, wherever you are.

I small chicken, well cleaned
½ sweet pepper, sliced
2 tbsp soy sauce
I garlic clove, diced
I tbsp plain flour or cornflour
water
I spring onion or skellion, sliced
I tomato, chopped
2 tbsp all-purpose seasoning
I tsp coarse ground black pepper
cooking oil for frying

1. Cut the cleaned chicken into small pieces, wash, drain and place them in a bowl then add the soy sauce, black pepper, all-purpose

seasoning, garlic and sweet peppers. Leave them to marinate for half an hour.

2. Put a good amount of cooking oil into a dutchpot or large frying pan, remove the chicken pieces from the marinade then fry them until they are brown.

3. Set the browned chicken pieces aside and drain the excess oil from the pan.

4. Spoon in the sweet pepper and the marinade and fry gently in the pan together with the spring onion or skellion.

5. Add two cupfuls of boiling water to the pan and let it simmer.

6. Mix the flour with a little cold water until it makes a smooth paste and add it to the pan.

7. Allow the liquid in the pan to come to the boil and thicken slightly, then return the chicken pieces to the pan, cover, lower the heat and leave it to simmer in the rich sauce for 15-20 minutes.

Serve with rice or vegetables.

'Pommes d'Amour'

Plump, juicy tomatoes provide a bed for king prawns, dressed in Greek yoghurt.

½ skelllion or spring onion, thinly sliced	
2 large tomatoes	I small can chopped plum tomatoes
125g (4 oz) king prawns	I clove garlic, diced
2 tbsp olive oil	½ chilli pepper, chopped
2 tbsp Greek yoghurt	fresh parsley, finely chopped
salt and black pepper	

1. Wash and dry the 2 large tomatoes, then place them in an oven dish.

2. Heat the olive oil in a pan and gently fry onions together with the chilli pepper and garlic for 2 minutes.

3. Add the tinned tomatoes, then sprinkle with salt and black pepper.

4. Pour mixture around the tomatoes in the oven dish and bake in pre-heated oven at 190 C / 375 F / Gas Mark 5 for 10 minutes. Add the prawns to the oven dish and bake for another 10 minutes.

5. Remove from oven and slice the tomatoes in half from the top almost to the bottom, pull slightly apart and fill the gap with a tablespoon of Greek yoghurt, then spoon over the sauce and king prawns, then garnish with chopped parsley.

Serve with a rice dish.

SWEET TREATS

Chocolate Truffles

Sheer indulgence!

125g (4oz) plain chocolate
100g (3½ oz) unsalted butter
drinking chocolate powder

275g (10 oz) icing sugar, sifted
2 tbsp dark rum

1. Put a bowl over a saucepan of boiled water, then break the chocolate into small pieces and place them in the bowl.
2. Allow the water to simmer gently, stirring the chocolate until melted and smooth.
3. Remove the bowl from over the saucepan and beat in the icing sugar, melted butter and rum until smooth.
4. Form the mixture into little balls and roll them in the chocolate powder, then place the balls into sweet cases and leave them to harden for 2-3 hours.

Ginger & Coconut Drops

Little drops of paradise!

½ coconut, shelled and grated
20g (½ oz) stem ginger, diced
1 cinnamon stick

375g (12 oz) sugar
375 ml (12 fl oz) water

1. Mix the sugar, water and cinnamon in a saucepan and bring it to the boil over a medium heat until it thickens.
2. Remove the cinnamon stick and add the grated coconut and ginger, stirring until the mixture holds together but remains moist.
3. Remove from the heat and drop spoonfuls of the mixture onto greased paper, then leave the drops to set.
4. When set, place into sweet cases.

What am I?

My first is in salmon
But not in bream
My next is in chocolate
Though not in cream
My third is in vinegar
Also in veal
My fourth is in everything
Eaten with zeal
Put them altogether
And what will be there
Is the most precious gift
That two people can share.

(Answer = L.O.V.E.)

Food for thought

In order to grow and thrive, the human body needs constant nourishment. This it gets from a combination of things that help to keep the body healthy – like food, exercise and relaxation.

But the body is merely the physical manifestation of a human being. Encased within it is the soul; the essential life force that makes each one of us who we are.

Thus, in order to grow and thrive as a complete human being, the soul must also be nourished. Emotions are components of the soul. It is from these that the soul derives its nourishment. And the most vital of all the emotions is love.

All too often, love comes wrapped up in layers of complex packaging. But when we cut through the strings, ties and confining restraints that hold the package together, we find what lies at the core of this emotion. That is, quite simply, pleasure and joy in knowing that someone lives!

To feel warmth for another human being, to wish them well, to just be glad that they are alive, is to feel 'love' for that person.

Be it someone we know well, or a total stranger brought out alive from the scene of a disaster, the basic emotion is the same. It is not dependent on who the person is, nor on what they say or do.

This love comes with no conditions and has no price tag. It is given for free, regardless of whether or not anything is received in exchange.

This is 'love' in its purest form – uncut, untainted, uncontaminated.

Capable of enriching both the giver and the receiver, the most nutritious soul food, and the simplest of gifts, is LOVE.

INDEX OF DISHES

Grace and Sonia Bailey are sisters. Sonia is a food consultant and accomplished restaurant manager well known for her culinary expertise. Grace is a lecturer and pioneering researcher in sexual health, she has also been a TV host in light entertainment for Channel 4 and Yorkshire Television.

Gloria Nicol is a professional photographer whose work has appeared in many books and leading magazines.

Acknowledgements: Special thanks to Barry Sutherland and staff at Bentley Wildfowl and Motor Museum, Richard & Penny Tapsfield, and John Morgan.

Photographs were taken on location at Bentley House, Bentley Wildfowl and Motor Musuem, Halland, Nr Lewes, East Sussex; the Forest of Dean, Gloucester; and Speldhurst, Kent

Published by ANGELA ROYAL PUBLISHING LTD
Brambletye, Ewehurst Lane, Speldhurst, Kent TN3 0JX

First published December 1996
1 3 5 7 9 10 8 6 4 2

A CIP catalogue for this book is available from the British Library
ISBN 1899860 35 5

Design & typesetting by Nick Awde/Desert♥Hearts

Printed by The Guernsey Press Company Limited, Guernsey GY1 3BW